D0198153

Will My Life Ever Be the Same?

H. Norman Wright

HARVEST HOUSE PUBLISHERS
Eugene, Oregon 97402

Unless otherwise indicated, all Scripture verses are taken from the New American Standard Bible, © 1960, 1962, 1963, 1968, 1971, 1972, 1973, 1975, 1977, 1995 by The Lockman Foundation. Used by permission.

Verses marked NIV are taken from the Holy Bible: New International Version®. NIV®. Copyright © 1973, 1978, 1984 by the International Bible Society. Used by permission of Zondervan Publishing House. The "NIV" and "New International Version" trademarks are registered in the United States Patent and Trademark Office by International Bible Society.

Verses marked AMP are taken from The Amplified Bible, Old Testament, Copyright © 1965, 1987 by The Zondervan Corporation, and from The Amplified New Testament, Copyright © 1954, 1958, 1987 by The Lockman Foundation. Used by permission.

Verses marked NKJV are taken from the New King James Version, Copyright © 1982 by Thomas Nelson, Inc. Used by permission. All rights reserved.

Verses marked RSV are taken from the Revised Standard Version of the Bible, Copyright © 1946, 1952, 1971, by the Division of Christian Education of the National Council of the Churches of Christ in the U.S.A. Used by permission.

Verses marked TLB are taken from *The Living Bible,* © 1971. Used by permission of Tyndale House Publishers, Inc., Wheaton, Illinois 60189. All rights reserved.

Verses marked NCV are taken from *The Holy Bible, New Century Version,* Copyright © 1987, 1988, 1991 by Word Publishing, Nashville, TN 37214. Used by permission.

Cover by Paz Design Group, Salem, Oregon

WILL MY LIFE EVER BE THE SAME?

Copyright © 2002 by H. Norman Wright
Published by Harvest House Publishers
Eugene, Oregon 97402
Previously published as *Why Did This Happen To Me?* (Ann Arbor, Michigan: Servant Publications, 1999).

Library of Congress Cataloging-in-Publication Data

Wright, H. Norman.
    Will my life ever be the same? / H. Norman Wright.
      p. cm.
    Includes bibliographical references.
    ISBN 0-7369-1029-8
    1. Consolation. 2. Suffering—Religious aspects—Christianity. 3. Life-change events—Religious aspects—Christianity. I. Title.
    BV4905.3.W74 2002
    248.8'6—dc21   2001059376

Printed in the United States of America.

02 03 04 05 06 07 08 09 10 11 / DP-MS / 10 9 8 7 6 5 4 3 2 1

Contents

Preface

Life is predictably unpredictable. One day everything is going along just fine—and then something unexpected crosses our path and knocks us off our feet. At such times, we think we're alone in the world and that no one can possibly help us feel right about life again. We ask ourselves, "Will my life ever be the same?" "Can I ever hope again?"

During my many years of counseling, I've heard story after story from men and women who underwent the most agonizing circumstances imaginable. They asked me those questions, with doubt in their voices. And just as I've told them, so I tell you: Yes, you can hope again. You will survive.

Sometimes I'm asked, "Is it possible to prevent or bypass these crises and traumas of life?" And I must answer, *no*. We must all pass through hard times. Not one of us is exempt.

Is it possible to survive them and even grow stronger because of them? *Yes*. And that's what this book is about. It's not just *surviving* our crises and traumas, but learning to let

God use them to make us stronger in our dependence upon Him.

Oh, you'll cry out and ask, "Why?" We all do. It's often our initial response when a crisis occurs. But in time, our cry of protest will change as we learn to understand the meaning of our time of pain.

That's what this book is about—helping you to understand the meaning of life's crises and traumas so you can truly be more than a survivor.

It *is* possible to rebound when life's storms knock you down. You *can* hope again.

1

"Why Did This Happen to Me?"

Understanding the Meaning of Crisis

All eyes were glued to the young man who stood poised just two inches from the edge of a platform more than two hundred feet in the air. From his perspective the distance probably seemed as deep as the abyss of the Grand Canyon. The people on the ground looked on with quiet fascination, waiting...just waiting. The man lifted one foot a few inches in the air, hesitated, and put it back down. Then he took a deep breath, blinked his eyes, and stepped out into space. Down and down he fell until his tether stretched taut. All of a sudden he seemed to rocket back up toward the platform. The elasticity of the bungee shot him skyward. It had resilience. It had the ability to bounce back.

One of the toys I remember from my childhood was a paddle with a long elastic band and a small rubber ball attached to it. You hit the little ball with the paddle as hard as you could to make it fly out as far as possible, stretching the elastic band to its limit. Let me tell you, it had resilience! Sometimes that ball came flying back at me like a missile, and all too frequently it missed the paddle and hit me! I quickly learned to respect the power of elasticity.

Over the years I've discovered that some people have the capability of bouncing back from adversity—they have *resilience*. But others don't. Perhaps you've wondered, as I have, what makes the difference. Why is it that some people have the ability to bounce back after a crisis while others don't? That is the purpose of this book—to discover the way not only to survive, but to *grow* through life's problems.

Stories of survival are all around us. The *Reader's Digest* has carried many of them. One issue told the story of four fishermen from a Central American country. One day as they were fishing, something happened to their boat. It just wouldn't work any more. Soon they were caught in the currents and swept out of sight of land and the shipping lanes. The men were adrift for months before they were discovered still alive. The focus of the article was on how they survived.

A newspaper carries the story of a plane crash in the mountains during the heart of winter. The combination of the snowstorms and the rugged terrain prevented rescuers from getting to the plane for ten days. Fearing the worst, they were amazed to discover 14 people still alive. One of the first questions the rescuers asked was, "How did you survive?"

Fortunately, most of us never face adversity so dramatic. And yet, when our crises hit, they are no less traumatic to us as we struggle through to the other side. For some people, the effort to overcome hard times seems endless as one tragedy barely ends before some new calamity presents itself. Then there are those who seem to be seldom visited by adversity. But then when it hits, it's such a shock they can't handle the enormity of it. The struggle to get their life back on track may be even harder for them than it is for those who are veterans in the war with adversity.

Right now you or a loved one may be in either situation. Your crisis could take the form of a devastating illness that destroys all the dreams you've been working toward for years. Your finances have been drained and the numbing ache of exhaustion and despair has crept into the life of your family. Perhaps you have a child who has run away from home or chosen a lifestyle totally in opposition of your values. Or maybe your situation is even as severe as the family whose eight-year-old girl was struck by a car as she rode her bicycle around a blind corner. This tragedy happened 25 years ago, and she still can't speak or move. Twenty-five years of waiting, hoping, and putting their dreams on hold.

Or consider one woman who, over the course of several years, saw two of her adult sons tragically killed, another son reveal his homosexuality, and her husband lose his memory of her due to a medical problem. This isn't fiction—it happened to Barbara Johnson; you may have read her story in one of her many best-selling books. In spite of all she's been through—and is still going through—*she's surviving.*

Many of you have probably watched the Superman films with Christopher Reeve playing the title role. The athletic actor liked to do some of his own stunts in the movies. But all that ended when one day his horse stopped at a jump during an equestrian competition. Because his hands were wrapped in the reins, Reeve couldn't put them out to break his fall. As a result, he became a "C1-C2," which is the designation for a paralyzing injury between the neck and the brain stem. It's called the "hangman's injury," since the break is the same as that in an execution when the scaffold trapdoor opens and the noose snaps tight. Christopher Reeve went from performing high-risk stunts, skiing, sailing, and riding in competitions to being strapped into a wheelchair—for the rest of his life. He is paralyzed, but he's busy. He has become a spokesperson for those who have undergone similar tragedies. *Christopher Reeve is surviving.*

I enjoy receiving not just cards at Christmas but also the newsletters telling of the year's events. One friend's letter recounted her year as follows:

- Nine of her friends from church were diagnosed with cancer and two subsequently died.

- She and her husband were involved in a head-on collision with another car.

- Her husband had kidney stone surgery with complications.

- Her father died.

- Two friends were sentenced to life in prison, one for poisoning his wife and the other for sexually molesting his granddaughter.

- Her brother-in-law left his wife and young child for cocaine.

- Her own brother was suicidal and finally entered an AA program.

- She was having lunch on an ocean pier with a student from Japan when an elderly man in a wheelchair wheeled himself to the end of the pier near them, lifted himself over the rail, and plunged into the ocean in an attempt to kill himself.

You're probably thinking, "That's unbelievable" or "It's too much for one person or family to handle" or "What an overload!" And that's what it was—overload. *But she's surviving.*

No Matter the Tragedy—Our Pain Is Real

On September 11, 2001, most of us began our day like any other. But by the day's end, our lives were changed forever as we watched the news reports recounting the terrorist attacks on our country that killed over 3000 people. For the tens of thousands of people who knew and loved one of the victims of the terrorists, life was profoundly altered that day. During the months that followed that horrific devastation, I flew to New York and met with many who had lost loved ones that day. Their pain and our nation's pain will be with us for years. (The tragedy of September 11 will be discussed further in a later chapter.)

Your crisis may or may not make the nightly news. It may or may not be as severe as Barbara Johnson's, Christopher Reeve's, or my friend's. But to you, it's just as painful.

There are so many life-crushing events—the loss of a job, the loss of a spouse through divorce or death, abuse, lawsuit, mental illness in your family, being robbed or victimized in other ways. You know what I'm talking about; you can't help but know. The upsets of life are all around us.

Why is it that some people survive the crises and traumas of life, yet others don't? Why do some overcome the storms of life while others are overwhelmed by them?

Perhaps it's because we think of storms as exceptions to the rule of calm weather. Maybe our perspective is wrong. I propose that times of calm are more likely the exceptions.

Out of Nowhere and at the Wrong Time

A number of years ago I went fishing on a lake in Minnesota with several relatives. It was a beautiful day. As the afternoon wore on, it became very calm and still. Suddenly my cousin said, "Let's head for shore...quick!" I couldn't believe what I was hearing. The weather was great and the fish were beginning to bite. But my cousin said, "Just wait."

By the time we made the shoreline, ten minutes later, we were fighting 30 to 40 mile-per-hour winds. They seemed to come out of nowhere. For hours we huddled in our tents just waiting for them to be torn from their pegs.

Where did the storm come from? I wondered. One moment the sky was clear, the next we were being buffeted about by strong winds and a torrential rainstorm.

Storms are like that. They often appear out of nowhere at the "wrong time," usually when it's most inconvenient. They disrupt our plans and some leave devastation in their path. Life is never the same after some storms have swept through our lives.

There are other storms that do give us some warning. They appear gradually and the weather forecasters are able to give us some indication in advance. To some degree we can prepare for these tempests if the predictions are consistent and accurate. But often they aren't, and once again we find ourselves unprepared.

Storms come in all kinds, sizes, shapes, and intensities. There are rainstorms, firestorms, hailstorms, snowstorms, and windstorms. Nahum the prophet said, "[The Lord's] way is in the whirlwind and the storm" (1:3b NIV).

I've been in some storms where the sky was split open by flashing brilliant fingers of lightning followed by ear-deafening thunder. I've stood on the shoreline of Jackson Lake in the Grand Teton National Park and heard the thunder begin to roll through the Teton range 20 miles to the left of me and continue in front of me on up into Yellowstone National Park. It was a breathtaking, awesome experience.

Some storms are so new and different that we aren't sure just what to do when they hit. This was brought home to me in a dramatic way. Southern California, where my wife Joyce and I live, is not known for having tornadoes. We have rain, Santa Ana winds, earthquakes, and hot weather, but no tornadoes...until a few years ago when we experienced a full-sized twister on our own street. I wasn't home; Joyce was.

While she was working in the yard, she began to feel some strange and strong winds. Realizing that something was wrong, she went inside and shut the door. The winds continued, and it seemed as though the air was being sucked out of the house by this wind. She didn't know exactly what was happening, so she shut herself in one of the rooms.

About this time a neighbor turned the street corner in time to see the twister touch down in the middle of the block and begin coming toward her. She drove her car into her garage and ran inside the house just before the tornado ripped a large tree from her front yard.

We were fortunate. No homes were lost, but several trees were uprooted. I guess the worst part was that this was trash day, and in front of each home were several full trash cans. After the tornado hit they were all empty! Everyone in our neighborhood was amazed, surprised, stunned. This just doesn't happen in our area. No one knew what to do!

As unpredictable as some weather can be, we can usually tolerate it. But it's the storms of life that throw us.

Crises Are a Normal Part of Life

Some storms are predictable, some give us a bit of warning, and others penetrate our plans and our lives like the attack of an alien invader. We can't avoid them, *but we can handle them in such a way that they don't cripple or devastate us for the remainder of our lives.*

When we experience a crisis, it seems as though everything is "on the line." Webster defines crisis as a "crucial time" and "a turning point in the course of anything." The term *crisis* is often used to describe a person's internal response to some external hazard. When you or I experience a crisis, at first we are thrown off guard and temporarily lose our ability to cope.

But we can quickly regain our footing in a crisis if we understand what a crisis is and the potential that lies within it for our benefit. Far too often we think of crises as the unusual, mostly negative, events we should avoid—when they are actually the stuff of which life is made. Why do I say that? Because crises, handled correctly, have the potential for developing Christian character in us in a way that few of life's events can do.

At first, it's difficult to see any potential, any good, any benefit, or even any way to recover from the crisis. You can look at the front page of the newspaper or watch the first 15 minutes of a newscast to see that crises come in all shapes and sizes.

A businessman who lost his business and had to declare bankruptcy lost his vision for his future. He wondered if life would ever be stable again. Not only did he repeatedly ask why, but he also wondered where God was when he needed Him the most. His crisis challenged his beliefs and faith in God. *How could such a loss have any purpose?* he thought. He felt at loose ends, wondering what his first step would be to move forward. The crushing experience immobilized him.

I can think of a more public example. Perhaps you remember a significant day in sports. One of the best hitters for the Montreal Expos was at the plate facing a hard-throwing pitcher for the San Francisco Giants. The pitcher looked at the runner at first base and then threw as hard as he could. Little did he know it was the last pitch he would ever throw in any kind of game. A sharp crack was heard all over the stadium as the bone in Dave Dravecky's arm snapped in two. Those watching saw him grasp his arm; later he said that he'd felt it was going to fly toward home plate. They also heard his scream as he fell to the ground.

It wasn't that his arm was broken. The doctors found that the cancer he thought was in remission had reappeared. His arm would have to be amputated at the shoulder to ensure the cancer wouldn't spread to the rest of his body.[1]

Can you imagine the questions and thoughts that would run through your mind if you had just gone through this experience? You're losing part of your body. You're losing the skill you've worked for years to perfect. You're probably asking yourself, *What about my identity? What if the cancer spreads? What are my odds of surviving? How will I make a living now?* Numbness, fear, and dread soon become your companions.

Consider the plight of all the parents of runaway children or teens on drugs. These parents know what a crisis is.

I think of a friend of mine who was driving home from work when he came upon an accident. A car had hit a motorcycle. My friend stopped and went over to the car to see if the occupants were all right. They were. He then walked toward the downed motorcycle and felt a subtle sense of recognition within. As he stepped over the green motorcycle and lifted the visor of the rider's helmet, he looked into the face of his 19-year-old son—who was dead. His entire family entered into the worst crisis a parent can imagine.

When you lose a loved one, there's a large aching hole in your life. Your sense of disbelief coupled with the numbness soon evolves to the pain of realizing that the person is dead...gone *forever.* My friend felt as though part of him had been cut away when the full reality of his son's death hit him. He thought, *My son will never come through that door again with a smile on his face.* Any future with his son had been destroyed.

I read the personal story of a professor's nightmare as he described it in his book, *A Grace Disguised:*

> We returned to our van, loaded and buckled up, and left for home. By then it was dark. Ten minutes into our trip home I noticed an oncoming car on a lonely stretch of highway driving extremely fast. I slowed down at a

curve, but the other car didn't. It jumped its lane and smashed head-on into our minivan. I learned later that the alleged driver was drunk, driving 85 miles per hour. He was accompanied by his pregnant wife, also drunk, who was killed in the accident.

I remember those first moments after the accident as if everything was happening in slow motion. They are frozen into my memory with a terrible vividness. After recovering my breath, I turned to survey the damage. The scene was chaotic. I remember the look of terror on the faces of my children and the feeling of horror that swept over me when I saw the unconscious and broken bodies of Lynda, my four-year-old daughter Diana Jane, and my mother. I remember getting Catherine (then eight), David (seven), and John (two) out of the van through my door, the only one that would open. I remember taking pulses, doing mouth-to-mouth resuscitation, trying to save the dying and calm the living. I remember the feeling of panic that struck my soul as I watched Lynda, my mother, and Diana Jane all die before my eyes. I remember the pandemonium that followed: people gawking, lights flashing from emergency vehicles, a helicopter whirring overhead, cars lining up, medical experts doing what they could to help. And I remember the realization sweeping over me that I would soon plunge into a darkness from which I might never again emerge as a sane, normal, believing man.

In the hours that followed the accident, the initial shock gave way to an unspeakable agony. I felt dizzy with grief's vertigo, cut off from family and friends, tormented by the loss, nauseous from the pain. After arriving at the hospital, I paced the floor like a caged animal, only recently captured. I was so bewildered that I was unable to voice questions or think rationally. I felt wild with fear and agitation, as if I was being stalked by some deranged killer from whom I could not escape. I could not stop crying. I could not silence the deafening noise of crunching metal, screaming sirens, and wailing children. I could not rid my eyes of the vision of violence, of shattering glass and broken bodies. All I wanted was to be dead. Only the sense of responsibility for my three surviving children and the habit of living for 40 years kept me alive.[2]

This wasn't just a crisis. It was *traumatic*. Part of this man's life had been amputated. Any time we lose something tangible, we also lose something intangible, but just as real.

Every family has their story of crisis events. Some are severe above and beyond anything that any of us should have to experience. The recovery from these traumatic events seems to go on forever.

Crisis Kills Our Dreams

With most crises comes another unwelcome guest—the death of a dream. Perhaps one of the best expressions of what we experience when this happens comes from the poet Langston Hughes:

> ...if dreams die
> life is a broken-winged bird

that cannot fly.
…when dreams go
life is a barren field
frozen with snow.[3]

I'm sure Sue felt all the emotion inherent in this poem when something happened to devastate her life. Sue was a woman who had a threefold dream: being a wife, a mother, and a missionary. She achieved all three. It seemed as though all her dreams were coming true. She had a husband and two girls, and she was serving on a foreign mission field. Then one day she discovered her husband had been involved in an affair. With that knowledge, everything changed. She now lives in the U.S., works as a nurse, and is rearing her girls alone. She tells about the death of her dream:

> There were actually two dreams that died when my husband walked out. One of them was the death of a marriage. I had this vision that I was going to be married for the rest of my life. Now that vision was gone. For a long time I had a mental picture that I was standing at a grave, trying to bury my marriage. The hole was dug, but boards were across the grave so they couldn't continue the burial because I refused to throw in my flowers. I was holding a dead wedding bouquet, my symbol of my marriage. I hung on to that bouquet for a long time.
>
> I knew I was beginning to heal when the day came in my vision that I wanted to pick up some fresh pink carnations for myself and throw the dead bouquet into the casket. That's when I knew I was beginning to let go of my grief.[4]

Building New Dreams

We need to grieve over destroyed dreams. But there's something else that can happen to a dream. When it doesn't die, yet is damaged, the dream is altered. Then we must begin building our dream anew.

I dreamed that my daughter would attend college. After all, I had almost nine years of college and graduate school behind me! But there was another reason I had such high expectations for Sheryl. Our son, Matthew, was profoundly retarded and would never be more than an infant mentally. This added to my desire that Sheryl go to college. Plus, I taught at a Christian university at the time and her tuition would be free.

After one year of college Sheryl said it wasn't for her. After half of a semester at fashion design school she dropped out and said she was going to cosmetology school to become a manicurist. Our initial dream was damaged and we wondered where this new unexpected dream would lead. Little did we know what would happen!

Today Sheryl is one of the leading nail technicians and nail artists in the nation! She has won most of the national and international nail competitions. She has published her own nail art books, and is asked to teach and judge events in this country as well as internationally. She has products in Wal-Mart and K-Mart and has illustrated two of my books. She has reached *her* dreams. Our dreams needed to be altered to line up with hers. *There are times when we all need to accept altered dreams in order to move ahead.*

Throughout your city or town right now, many people are experiencing their own world-collapsing crises:

> A young man's heart, which had become a receptacle for love for a certain young lady, is now filled with pain he could never have imagined because she said no to his marriage proposal.

- A family has had no income for months. The unemployment checks have run out and there are no prospects for a job.

- A young athlete who has spent 15 years working toward his dream of playing professional ball hears the surgeon say, "Your knee injury is beyond repair."

- A young mother who has gone to check on her three-month-old baby finds that he's a victim of SIDS (Sudden Infant Death Syndrome).

- A 40-year-old man who has just walked out of the doctor's office in a dazed fog is still trying to make sense of the deadly prognosis he's just heard.

- A wife said goodbye to her husband as he boarded a flight in Boston on September 11. Two hours later he and over three thousand others were dead.

The crises you and I experience can be the result of one event or of several. The crisis may be great or overwhelming, such as the death of a child, or it could be a problem that has a special significance just for you that makes it overwhelming. The crisis could be a problem that comes at a time of special vulnerability or when you're unprepared. I'm sure you've had to handle a stopped-up sink. Usually this presents no real difficulty except for the inconvenience. But if the sink stops up when you've had the flu and little or no sleep for two nights, you feel overwhelmed. It's the last straw!

If a problem occurs when your coping abilities are not functioning well, or when you don't have the support or help from others that you need, you can feel overwhelmed and see the event as a crisis.

There are three possible outcomes of a crisis: a change for the better, a change for the worse, or a return to the previous level of functioning. The word *crisis* is rich with meaning. The Chinese term for *crisis (weji)* is made up of two symbols: one is for danger and the other for opportunity. The English word is based on the Greek word *(krinein),* meaning "to decide." Crisis is a time of decision and judgment as well as a turning point during which there will be a change for the better or worse.

When a doctor talks about a crisis, he is talking about the moment in the course of a disease when a change for the better or worse occurs. When a counselor talks about a marital crisis, he or she is talking about the turning point when the marriage can go in either direction; it can move toward growth, enrichment, and improvement, or it can move toward dissatisfaction, pain, and in some cases, dissolution. As you think of the crises you've experienced, ask yourself, "How did they turn out?" A change for the better, for the worse, back to normal, or a redefinition of normal?

Crisis is not always bad; it can become a turning point in your life for the better. Yes, it can bring danger and upset, but it also carries with it opportunity for growth and change. As you try to discover a way to cope with your present crisis, you may discover a new and better way of living.

"Get Me Out of This!"

Coping with the Inevitability of Crisis

Crisis. What is it specifically? How do you know when you're in crisis?

Four elements work together to make up this undesired experience. When you're aware of these four elements and understand how they contribute to the crisis state, you take the first step toward handling life's crises in a more positive manner.

The first element is a *sudden upsetting event*. This can be anything that starts a chain reaction of events, which in turn leads to crisis. For example,

- A young wife who prepared for her career for seven years now discovers she is unexpectedly pregnant.

- A college senior who gave himself to basketball during school in order to play in the NBA shatters an ankle while hiking.

- A widower who is raising five preadolescent children loses his job in a very specialized profession.

What these people have in common is an event that disrupts their goals or livelihood.

Whenever you find yourself getting upset or having difficulty coping, ask yourself, "What event is occurring or has just occurred in my life?" The cause of your upset is usually fairly obvious.

The second element contributing to a crisis is *your vulnerability*. Not all negative events lead to crisis. You have to be vulnerable in some way for a crisis to occur. For example, if you go without sleep for a couple of nights, you could be vulnerable to a situation you usually handle without difficulty. Illness and depression also lower a person's coping ability, as do unresolved emotional issues from the past.

Recently, I talked with a woman who wanted to give up her foster child, cancel an important fund-raising event, and quit her business. Why? Because she was depressed over the possibility of another loss in her life. She was overwhelmed and felt like giving up everything! I asked her not to make any life-changing decisions during her time of depression because she might regret those decisions later on.

The third element in a crisis is *the actual precipitating factor*. You know—the last straw! These are the times when you seem to cope with one upsetting event after another, then go to pieces when you drop a piece of food on your clothes. In reality, your reaction to dropping the food is a reaction to all of the other events. It's like saving up all of your upsets and dumping the whole load when a family member does something you don't like. Out comes all the accumulated anger at once. Most, if not all, of the anger is about things completely unrelated to what your family member just did.

The last element is *the state of crisis*. Everyone differs in the way he or she handles a crisis. If I were to ask how you respond to crisis, what would you say? When you feel that you can no longer handle what is happening in your life, then it becomes a crisis. There are several indications of this state.

Usually there are actual symptoms of stress, which include physiological or psychological factors, or both. These symptoms can include depression, anxiety, headaches, or even bleeding ulcers. In other words, you experience some type of extreme discomfort.

You also experience a sense of panic or defeat. You may feel as though you've tried everything, and nothing works. You feel like a failure: defeated, overwhelmed, helpless. Hope? There *is* no hope as far as you're concerned.

At this point you can respond in one of two ways: You can become agitated and engage in behavior that's actually counterproductive—pacing back and forth, taking drugs, driving too fast, getting into arguments or fights. The other response is to become apathetic—which is equally counterproductive. This apathy could include excessive sleeping or drinking to the extent that you no longer feel the pain.

Your main concern at this time is getting some relief. *"Get me out of this!"* you want to scream. We want relief from the pain of the stress—and we want it *now*. Instead, we wait— for others, for relief, or for God to respond to our prayers and change our situation.

In a major crisis we're not in a condition to resolve our problems in a rational manner. This adds to our state of confusion, since we're usually capable of functioning quite well. Shock makes a person appear dazed and respond in bizarre ways. If you're in shock, you may feel frantic and look to other people for help. In fact, you may become very dependent on others to help you out of the dilemma.

This is also a time of decreased efficiency. You may continue to function normally, but instead of responding at 100 percent capability, your response may be at 60 percent. This, too, disturbs you. The greater you perceive the threat of your crisis, the less ability you will have to cope.

To Be or Not to Be a Crisis

Although most crises are unavoidable and come upon us suddenly, others may begin as minor problems that eventually escalate into a crisis.

There are three factors that affect the intensity of a crisis and may even contribute to an event becoming a crisis: how you view a problem, how much support you have from others, and how strong your coping mechanisms are.

First let's consider *the way you view a problem*. Some difficulties would be threatening for anyone, whereas some would be threatening *just for you*. Sometimes it's your perception that makes the event threatening. Your beliefs, ideas, expectations, and perceptions all work together as you determine whether or not a situation is a crisis.

We all have our own way of looking at an event. Two people can view the same event differently, depending on several factors. For instance, you appraise the death of a close friend from several viewpoints: how close the relationship was, how often you were in touch with that friend, how you have responded to other losses, and how many losses you have experienced recently. A woman deeply involved in her husband's life perceives his death differently than does a close friend, a business associate, or the uncle who saw the deceased once every five years.

When you experience a crisis, you are perceiving the loss or threatened loss of something important to you. Think of what is most important to you. Is there anything in your life right now in danger of turning into a crisis? If you're having trouble formulating an answer, perhaps the following scenario can help you discover what is most important to you in your home life:

> You've been informed that your house is going
> to be completely destroyed in ten minutes.
> You have time to make two trips out of your

home, taking with you what is most important and valuable to you. What will you take?

People are often surprised at what has meaning for them and what doesn't. This exercise also causes some people to reevaluate what they feel is important. Consider another scenario.

What one event, were it to occur in the next 12 months, would be the most upsetting or devastating to you? List the next four events in order of importance, using the same criteria. Now think about how you would handle those events and work through the loss involved in each one.

Did you know that even a job promotion can precipitate a crisis? Take Ralph, for example. Ralph was a car salesman who was promoted to sales manager. This gave him more status, more money, and more changes in his relationships. He was no longer on the same level as the other salesmen and now had to push and urge them to make their sales quotas. He was uncomfortable in this role and became so dissatisfied that he began to call in sick to avoid the pressure and conflicts. His loss of confidence threw him into a crisis.

A second factor that affects the intensity of a crisis is the support of our network of friends, relatives, or agencies. This is where the body of Christ—the church—should come into play as one of the greatest support groups available. But the church needs to know how to respond at such a time. I know of several churches that respond to a person or family's loss of a loved one by having a different family assigned to minister to them each week for a year. They call the family, send notes, deliver food, take them out, and so on.

A third factor that helps determine whether an event becomes a crisis or not involves a person's coping mechanisms. If your coping mechanisms do not function well, or they break down quickly, then crisis is inevitable. Some coping mechanisms are healthy, while others are destructive. Coping mechanisms run the gamut—rationalization, denial, researching what others say, praying, reading Scripture, and more. The greater the number and diversity of *healthy* coping methods a person employs, the less likely it is that a problem or event will become a crisis.

Typical Responses to Crisis

When you experience a crisis, your response may differ from that of family members or friends. However, there are some basic responses common to all people, depending on what comforts them during difficult times. Take a look at some typical responses and see if you can identify how you respond to a crisis.

- Some individuals look for others to protect and control them at a time of crisis. They say, "Please take over for me."

- Some need a person who will help them maintain contact with what is real and what isn't. They say, "Help me know that I am real at this time. Help me know what is going on right now."

- Some feel terribly empty and need loving contact with others. They say, "Care for me; love me."

- Some need another person to be available at all times in order to feel secure. They say, "Always be by my side. Never leave."

- Some have an urgent need to talk. They say, "Let me get this off my chest. Listen to me again and again."

🔊 Some need advice on certain pressing matters. They say, "Tell me what to do."

🔊 Some need to sort out their conflicting thoughts. They say, "Help me put things into perspective."

🔊 Some need the assistance of some type of specialist. They say, "I need some professional advice."

Perhaps you identify with some of these responses. If so, why not share your need with those closest to you? When a crisis hits, it will help you feel more in control and keep you from feeling overwhelmed.

Those Who Flounder

Why do some people seem to handle crisis well, while others don't? Let's consider some characteristics of those who appear to have the most difficulty handling a crisis.

🔊 Some individuals are *emotionally fragile* to begin with, and specific events are more difficult for them to handle.

🔊 Those who have a *physical ailment or illness* will struggle because they have fewer resources upon which to draw.

🔊 Those who *deny reality* have a hard time coping with a crisis. Some may deny the fact that they are seriously ill or financially ruined or that their child is on drugs or has a terminal illness.

🔊 Dr. Ralph Hirschowitz, a Harvard psychiatrist, has created a term for the next characteristic. He calls it "magic of the mouth," which is the tendency to eat, drink, smoke, and talk excessively. When a crisis enters these people's lives, they seem to regress into self-medication through their mouths. They feel uncomfortable unless they're doing something with their mouths most of the time, such as eating, talking, smoking. This *refusal to face the real problem* can continue after the crisis is over and can actually help to create an additional crisis for the person.

❧ Another characteristic is an *unrealistic approach to time*. Some people crowd the time dimensions of a problem or they extend the time factors way into the future. They want the problem to be "fixed" right away, or they delay addressing it. Delay avoids the discomfort of reality, but enlarges the problem.

❧ People who struggle with *excessive guilt* will have difficulty coping with a crisis. They tend to blame themselves for the difficulty, which increases feelings of guilt, which further immobilizes them.

❧ People who place blame have a difficult time coping with a crisis. They do not focus on what the problem is, they focus on *"who caused the problem."* Their approach is to find enemies, either real or imagined, and project blame on them.

❧ Another characteristic of those who do not cope well with crisis is the tendency to be *overly dependent or overly independent*. Such people either turn away from offers of help or become clinging vines. Those who cling tend to suffocate those who are helping them. Overly independent people shun offers of help. They do not cry out for help, even if they're sliding toward disaster. When the disaster hits, they either continue to deny it or blame others for its occurrence.

❧ One other characteristic has a bearing upon all others: *how a person perceives God*.

Where Is God During a Crisis?

Our belief in God and how we perceive God—our theology—will affect how we cope with crisis. Our lives are based upon our theology, yet many people are frightened by it.

Many times when we go through difficult upsets and crises we are forced to reevaluate what we truly believe. Unfortunately, many people determine what they believe by what they are going through. They allow their theology to be determined by their circumstances. When they hit the problems of life, they seem to negate the promises of God and begin to wonder if He cares!

Sometimes a crisis changes our view of God. Max Lucado describes the process well:

> There is a window in your heart through which you can see God. Once upon a time that window was clear. Your view of God was crisp. You could see God as vividly as you could see a gentle valley or hillside. The glass was clean, the pane unbroken.
>
> You knew God. You knew how he worked. You knew what he wanted you to do. No surprises. Nothing unexpected. You knew that God had a will, and you continually discovered what it was.
>
> Then, suddenly, the window cracked. A pebble broke the window. A pebble of pain.
>
> Perhaps that stone struck when you were a child and a parent left home—forever. Maybe the rock hit in adolescence when your heart was broken. Maybe you made it into adulthood before the window was cracked. But then the pebble came.

> Was it a phone call? "We have your daughter at the station, you'd better come down."
>
> Was it a letter on the kitchen table? "I've left. Don't try to reach me. Don't try to call me. It's over. I just don't love you any more."
>
> Was it a diagnosis from the doctor? "I'm afraid our news is not very good."
>
> Was it a telegram? "We regret to inform you that your son is missing in action."[1]

Why do we end up feeling disappointed by God? Is it really because of Him, or could it be because of our own expectations? We have our own unexpressed agenda. We believe, "If God is God, then…" But does our agenda match the teaching of Scripture? Those who believe in the sovereignty and caring nature of a loving God have a better basis upon which to approach life—and to deal with crisis.

A book that has spoken to me every time I've read it is Lewis Smedes' *How Can It Be All Right When Everything Is All Wrong?* He has been through life's tough times. His insights and sensitivity to life's crises and God's presence and involvement in our lives can answer many of our questions. One of his personal experiences describes how our theology helps us move through life's changes.

> The other night, trying to sleep, I amused myself by trying to recall the most happy moments of my life. I let my mind skip and dance where it was led. I thought of leaping down from a rafter in a barn, down into a deep loft of sweet, newly mown hay. That was a superbly happy moment. But somehow my mind was also seduced to a scene some years ago that, as I recall it, must have been the most painful of my life.

Our firstborn child was torn from our hands by what felt to me like a capricious deity I did not want to call God. I felt ripped off by a cosmic con-artist. And for a little while, I thought I might not easily ever smile again.

But then, I do not know how, in some miraculous shift in my perspective, a strange and inexpressible sense came to me that my life, our lives were still good, that is good because it is *given*, and that its possibilities were still incalculable. Down into the gaps of feeling left over from the pain came a sense of givenness that nothing explains. It can only be felt as a gift of grace. An irrepressible impulse of blessing came from my heart to God for his sweet gift. And that was joy...in spite of pain. Looking back, it seems to me now that I have never again known so sharp, so severe, so saving a sense of gratitude and so deep a joy, or so honest.[2]

Chuck Swindoll always shares so realistically and helpfully about life's difficulties. He tells us how a crisis can impact us:

Crisis crushes. And in crushing, it often refines and purifies. You may be discouraged today because the crushing has not yet led to a surrender. I've stood beside too many of the dying, ministered to too many of the broken and bruised to believe that crushing is an end in itself. Unfortunately, however, it usually takes the brutal blows of affliction to soften and penetrate hard hearts. Even though such blows often seem unfair.[3]

Alexander Solzhenitsyn's admission illustrates what Chuck Swindoll is saying:

> It was only when I lay there on rotting prison straw that I sensed within myself the first stirring of good. Gradually, it was disclosed to me that the line separating good and evil passes, not through states, nor between classes, nor between political parties either, but right through all human hearts. So, bless you, prison, for having been in my life.[4]

Solzhenitsyn's words provide a perfect illustration of the psalmist's instuction to us in Scripture:

> Before I was afflicted I went astray,
>   but now I obey your word...
> It was good for me to be afflicted
>   So that I might learn from your decrees.
>
> PSALM 19:67,71 NIV

After crisis crushes sufficiently, God steps in to comfort and teach.

It's true that once crisis hits, life will never be exactly the way it was! A crisis is like a bomb that sprays its lethal projectiles all around without regard for anyone standing in its way. The haunting words of an old children's game reflect the fallout of a crisis.

> Ring around the rosie
> Pocketful of posies
> Ashes, ashes
> All fall down

But if we let Him, God uses the fallout from crisis to refine and hone our sense of His love toward us and His sovereignty in our lives.

The feelings you experience in a crisis come as waves. The earthquake intensity of any crisis eventually recedes, and then the tidal waves of emotions begin their hammering process. And they keep rolling in, wave after wave.

These feelings have to have an outlet. If not, they won't stay buried. One day they will explode with a vengeance. One author describes it well:

> I will never forget the time my dad left a can of aerosol spray in the back window of the family car while he was playing golf. The sun pounded on the window for a couple of hours and then the can detonated, shattering the windows and slicing a hole in the steel roof of the car. The force was unimaginable.
>
> It's the same way with unexpressed feelings born in the midst of crisis. They fester and fester until they explode, adding damage to damage, doing nothing to reduce the problem.[5]

The father who described the loss of three of his family members (p. 15) reflects on the turmoil of his feelings.

> Can anyone really expect to recover from such tragedy, considering the value of what was lost and the consequences of that loss? Recovery is a misleading and empty expectation. We recover from broken limbs, not amputations. Catastrophic loss by definition precludes recovery. It will transform us or destroy us, but it will never leave us the same. There is no going back to the past, which is gone forever, only going ahead to the future, which has yet to be discovered. Whatever that future is, it will, and must

> include the pain of the past with it. Sorrow
> never entirely leaves the soul of those who
> have suffered a severe loss. If anything, it
> may keep going deeper.
>
> But this depth of sorrow is the sign of a
> healthy soul, not a sick soul. It does not have
> to be morbid and fatalistic. It is not some-
> thing to escape but something to embrace.
> Jesus said, "Blessed are those who mourn,
> for they will be comforted." Sorrow indicates
> that people who have suffered loss are living
> authentically in a world of misery, and it
> expressed the emotional anguish of people
> who feel pain for themselves or for others.[6]

Perhaps this chapter has been reflective of some of your life experiences. Perhaps you've walked through a problem that turned into a crisis, and you now understand what factors led up to it and what intensified it. Or it could be that this chapter was a window into the future for you since your crises have yet to hit.

What Gerald Sittser said in the last quote is true: A crisis will either destroy us or transform us. Isn't it sad that the first lesson most of us learn about crisis is when we experience it? Why weren't we taught about the reality of crisis and its characteristics and so be prepared to handle crisis before it hits?

Those who recover from a crisis are the people who understand the meaning of crisis, the typical ways of responding to a crisis, and the stages a person will experience as he or she walks through it. As you read the next chapter you will realize that all you've experienced in your crisis times is *normal*. This knowledge not only brings a sense of relief, but also provides help with becoming a person of resilience.

"Am I Normal?"

Recognizing the Pattern of Crisis

Y ou open your eyes but you can't see clearly. You blink. Everything is hazy, as though you were in a thick fog. There's a sense of unreality in everything around you. You feel as though you've been run over by a three-ton truck. You blink again, but your view of the world is still a bit fuzzy. Are you losing your mind? Were you in an accident? Did someone hit you? Probably none of the above.

Welcome to the world of a crisis. When you and I enter into that state called "crisis time," we feel as though we've grabbed hold of a live electrical wire! And as difficult as our entry into a crisis may be, there are three more phases we will yet pass through. As you read about the four phases inherent in a crisis, keep in mind that the time to transition through each phase will vary for each individual. Don't compare your experience with the approximate time suggested for getting through each phase. You could experience an intense crisis or trauma that prolongs a certain phase for months. And if you face another crisis before resolving the first one, the situation is compounded, further delaying each phase.

Why is it important to know about the phases of a crisis? By knowing what the four phases are, you will

- ✍ realize that you're not going crazy—you're going through a normal passage,

- ✍ release some of the pain and pressure by recalling that, "Oh yes, this phase will pass and I'll go on to the next one,"

- ✍ recognize there's light at the end of the tunnel—there is hope,

- ✍ regain control of your life and the outcome a bit sooner by knowing what to expect.

As writer Ann Stearns put it:

> Recovery from loss is like having to get off the main highway every so many miles because the fire route is under reconstruction. The road signs reroute you through little towns you hadn't expected to visit and over bumpy roads you hadn't wanted to bounce around on. You are basically traveling in the appropriate direction. On the map, however, the course you are following has the look of shark's teeth instead of a straight line. Although you are gradually getting there, you sometimes doubt that you will ever meet up with the finished highway. There is a finished highway in your future. You won't know when or where, but it is there. You will discover a greater sense of resilience when you know in advance what you will experience and that you're normal in your response.[1]

The Impact Phase

The first stage of a crisis is called the impact phase. The intensity of a person's response to a crisis varies, but all of us feel the *impact* of a crisis. You know immediately that something drastic has happened to you. You're stunned. It's as if someone has hit you over the head with a two-by-four, and you're seeing stars.

In chapter 1 you read an account of a father who had been in a car accident that killed three family members. He described his feeling of horror and shock. He was in the impact phase when life appears to be falling apart with no hope for relief.

For some who see the crisis unfolding before them, there's a sense of panic and fear. This happens even to those who are observers of an impending crisis. The "Oh, no!" response is normal when you see a major tragedy about to occur, and there's nothing you can do to stop it. I've experienced this more than once.

Years ago I was driving home in the late afternoon from teaching my classes at the graduate school at Biola University. I turned onto Stage Road, which runs parallel to the Amtrak train tracks, and then made another turn onto a cross street. Because the train was due in less than a minute, the arms at the train crossing had come down on the cross street.

While waiting in line, several drivers became impatient and began to drive around the crossing arm and across the tracks. Out of the corner of my eye I saw the passenger train hurtling down the track as a VW Beetle began to sneak across. In that split second I knew what was going to happen. And with that knowledge I let out an anguished cry of "Oh, no!"

Then it happened. The train plowed into the small car and dragged the twisted metal hundreds of feet along the track. Turning my car out of the line of stopped traffic, I drove to a pay phone and called for help. As I drove home my mind and body were in shock. I think I prayed and talked out loud the entire way home.

When I got home I saw my wife and our daughter by the car. Sheryl had her driving permit and was getting into the driver's seat. I pulled up, got out of the car, and said to them, "Sheryl is *not* driving anywhere today!" then went into the house. They were shocked at my outburst and followed me inside. They found me in the family room, pacing back and forth. I started to tell them what had happened, expressing my horror through tears. It took some time for the crash images to lose their sense of reality.

The next day I learned that the driver of the car was a young Biola student and the daughter of one of the professors there. Fortunately she survived, although it took her months to recover.

Another time I had just walked into my bedroom and heard a helicopter flying overhead. The sound wasn't the normal pitch of the engine, so I rushed outside. I looked up and saw the helicopter twisting and turning as it flew on, apparently out of control. It continued to veer one way and then another as the pilot fought to maintain control. About a mile away, the helicopter plunged straight down. During this time, I was saying, "Oh, no! It can't be!" Part of my worry came from its proximity to a friend's home.

Later I learned that tragedy was averted when the craft hit wires that broke its fall. The three occupants escaped with minor injuries. But I still experienced that state of pain and panic.

In recalling a crisis experience in his own life, Gordon MacDonald wrote:

> I will never forget those first days. It was almost impossible to ward off the feeling that life was over, all that brightness and joy that

we had known for more than 45 years had come to a screeching halt.

Our worlds were broken. A dream had turned into a nightmare of loss, humiliation, anger and a sense of a very dark future. There was the terrific realization that many who had trusted me were now disillusioned. There was the knowledge that some people were talking, with or without a knowledge of the facts.

At one point I felt as though the ground was opening beneath me! Like if I were to look down the world was going to swallow me up.[2]

MacDonald isn't alone in his dramatic description of the crisis phase. Others have expressed it this way:

"I felt like I was in a free fall. But I didn't have a parachute!"

"It was a strange sensation. I sort of felt as though the world was somehow less real, like I was disconnected, except of course when it came crashing in on me. It was that kind of alternating experience: Sometimes I was 'out of it'; sometimes I was in the middle of it; but I could never go away from it."

"There was this growing sense of powerlessness."[3]

The Length of the Impact Phase

The impact phase is usually brief, lasting from a few hours to a few days, depending upon the event and the person involved. (There are some experiences that prolong this phase much longer). Some impact phases linger on and on, such as in the case of a divorce proceeding. If you can identify with the words of the previous examples, you may be in this phase now.

The more severe the crisis or loss, the greater the impact and the greater the amount of incapacitation and numbness. Tears may be an immediate part of this phase, or they may be expressed later on.

During this initial phase, one of the questions you must answer is, "Should I stay and face the problem or withdraw and run from it?" This is called the fight-or-flight pattern.

A few years back, an advertisement espoused the words, "I'd rather fight than switch." Not everyone feels that way in a crisis. If your tendency in the past has been to face problems, you will probably face your crisis head-on. But if your tendency has been to avoid or withdraw from problems, you will probably run from your next crisis. If the crisis is especially severe, you may feel like running anyway, because you're not as able to cope during the impact phase.

Most of the time, running from a crisis is not the solution. It merely prolongs the situation. You may not feel capable of facing this problem at first, but in time that will change.

Don't expect to do any clear thinking during the impact phase. You'll feel numb and disoriented. You may even feel as though you can't think or feel at all. Someone described it this way: "I feel as though my entire system shut down." Your short-term memory may diminish.

Your ability to process information is limited. If a friend or family member attempts to share any factual information with you, it sails right over your head. You may ask, "What did you say?" even though the person has repeated it for the third time. Don't despair when this happens. It's a normal response that everyone experiences.

It's best if you don't have to make any important decisions at this time, but if you do, ask a competent friend to help you.

At the heart of most crises is a loss of some kind. Losses threaten our security, our sense of stability, our well-being. Self-image may be affected, and you feel out of control. The more sudden the loss, the more out of control you will feel. Although a gradual loss is still painful, you can prepare for it to some degree. But a sudden, unexpected death or similar tragedy may disrupt your ability to activate the emotional resources you need in order to cope with the loss. The more sudden, unexpected, and tragic the event, the greater the impact.

Loss—A New Meaning

Since September 11, 2001, most Americans are learning to live with one of the most difficult losses to handle—threatened loss. These losses used to be reserved for the employees who read the memo stating there would be a 30 percent downscaling in their company. Those affected would be told in two weeks. Or the woman sitting in her doctor's office hearing those dreaded words, "There's a growth. I'll take a biopsy and we'll let you know the results in a week." It could be a spouse saying, "I'm thinking of divorcing you." It's one of the most difficult to deal with; it's waiting for a crisis to happen.

With a threatened loss you feel powerless, like a victim waiting for the bad news. There's nothing you can do. And the likelihood that you will experience this loss is high. That's why threatened losses are often the worst.

With the rise of terrorism in our land, we are all living under this threat to some degree. We wonder, *When will terrorists hit again? Where? How?* And so we're on edge, a bit suspicious, not as functional, somewhat subdued, sad and angry, waiting and wondering. I see it in those at church, at the store, in the counseling office, at the airport, and especially on the East Coast.

Anyone who lost a friend or family member in an attack such as occurred at the World Trade Center is struggling with yet another loss—ambiguous loss. Many have never heard about this classification. I hadn't until two years ago when I read a book on this subject.[4] Then when I saw the devastation at "Ground Zero" in New York City, amidst my own emotional response, the phrase *ambiguous loss* came to mind. As Pauline Boss said, "Of all the losses experienced in personal relationships, ambiguous loss is the most devastating because it remains unclear, indeterminate."[5] People want closure. They want to see the remains or a body. But for those who lost someone in New York or a field in Pennsylvania or at the Pentagon on that tragic day, their loved one may still be missing. Family members have to live with ambiguity and uncertainty. They want to know for certain. But they never will. Many worried relatives and friends called the phone companies to see if their loved one used their cell phone after the disaster. Perhaps there was hope after all, they thought. But there wasn't. Until there is closure, the lost person is still alive in the minds of their loved ones.

With this ambiguous loss people are baffled and immobilized. They have difficulty problem solving and may never be able to achieve the detachment that's necessary for normal closure.[6] There's an endless searching, hoping. This kind of loss can traumatize its victims. The loss continues, and a family alternates between hope and hopelessness. They deal with the death but want closure. The family is denied the rituals that support a tangible loss. Thus their grief is frozen.

This ambiguous loss impacted others throughout our country after the World Trade Center disaster. The deployment of our military troops is yet another expression of this loss since the families have no idea where their family member is going or how long they'll be gone.

This is the loss of an MIA, a runaway, or an adoptee searching for her birth parents. The variations of ambiguous loss are many.

What then can we do? For ourselves, we can face our own sense of threat and address any ambiguous loss in our life related or unrelated to events such as September 11, 2001. And when we're called upon to help others, we can help them look at their losses within a new framework.

Any kind of loss has a way of changing our lives in a dramatic way and affects the way we think about the future. These changes can be positive and eventually enrich our lives. But during the first few months of a crisis, it doesn't feel that way at all. If someone were to tell you during the impact phase of a loss that you can learn and grow through your circumstances, you might react with disgust, anger, or disbelief! You aren't ready to handle thoughts like that. You can only hear such comments when life is more stable.

During the impact phase, a person's thought life focuses on the loss in an effort to find what he or she has lost. It's normal to search for something that meant a great deal to you. You're trying to hold on to your emotional attachments for a bit longer. You're trying to recapture the lost dream, the loved one, or even your health. The more your loss meant to you, the more you will search!

This searching behavior often takes the form of reminiscing. How much you reminisce varies in proportion to the value of what you lost. It's common (and healthy) to pore over photographs and other items that remind you of the person who died.

Surviving the Impact

There are several things you can do to work through the impact stage of loss. In fact, the following action steps will help you deal with your grief in a healthy way. What do you need to do during the impact phase of a crisis?

1. *Accept what has happened and your feelings about it. Allow yourself to reminisce.* Recently I was counseling a young woman who had lost her father six months earlier. She flew to the eastern U.S. for the funeral, but had not gone back since. This meant that she had not had the opportunity to spend time in the home where her father lived or to reminisce with friends or other relatives. Because of this, her grief was blocked. I suggested that she write her mother and ask her to send the photograph album that contained pictures of her and her father. When it arrived, I encouraged her to sit down with a friend and look through the book and talk about the various experiences each picture portrayed. She needed to reminisce.

2. *Express as many feelings as you can.* It may be difficult at first to experience your feelings because of the numbness you feel, but when the numbness wears off, your feelings can be intense. This intensity may increase and carry into the next phase. You may even find yourself emotionally exhausted. Expressing your feelings is a normal and healthy way to release them in a positive way.

3. *You need a safe environment in which to grieve.* Avoid people who try to make you stifle your feelings. Feelings shouldn't be buried or denied at this point because rejected feelings delay the resolution of the problem. When feelings are buried, they don't go away; they are simply frozen. One day they will emerge—just when you least expect them to.

Do you know what happens to water when it freezes? It expands. Water frozen in steel pipes has the power to burst them wide open. When we lock up a summer mountain cabin for the winter, it's important to drain all of the water from the pipes if we want them to function properly the next spring. The analogy holds true when we speak of frozen emotions. They expand and take on a power out of proportion to their original nature. It's important during grief and crisis to keep the channels open so feelings can flow when they need to.

Avoid people who are full of advice and say, "I told you so" or "Spiritual Christians get over their hurt sooner than others." Find people who are empathetic and know how to minister to you during a crisis. The people who can help you most have these qualities:

- They don't shock easily, but accept your human feelings.

- They're not embarrassed by your tears.

- They don't give unwanted advice.

- They're warm and affectionate with you, according to your needs.

- They help you recall your strengths when you've forgotten you have strengths.

- They trust you to be able to come through this difficult time.

- They treat you like an adult who can make your own decisions.

- They may become angry with you, but they don't attack your character.

- They respect your courage and sense of determination.

- They understand that grief is normal, and they are acquainted with the stages of grief.

- They, too, may have been through times of difficulty and can share those times with you.

- They do not spiritualize everything.

      They are sensitive to where you are spiritually and don't try to force-feed you theology and Scripture.[7]

Cultivate friendships with these people *before* a crisis hits. But remember, we draw these people to us as we demonstrate *we* are that kind of person, too.

Some people talk to release their feelings because that's what they do best. Others may empty themselves of their emotions in physical ways. We shouldn't compare ourselves with others and say one way of release is the only or the best way. Some people talk about their hurt and grief; some act it out. You may have a friend who spends a great deal of time working in the yard or doing some kind of activity but doesn't talk about the loss of her spouse. You may be concerned that she's not dealing with her loss, but she may be doing just that in her own way.

For some, rigorous physical activity can bring about healing. I heard of a man who lost his father in a tragic fire. He lived near his father on an adjacent farm. One night the home in which he was born and raised burned to the ground with his father inside. His response to this tragedy startled other family members. He remained silent while they all wept and talked about the loss. Then he borrowed a bulldozer and proceeded to bulldoze the ashes and charred remains of the house.

The rain had stopped the fire, and this was his one expression of burying his father. He worked for hours, not even stopping for meals or rest. When darkness came, he continued to work, ignoring the requests of family members to stop for the night. Instead he continued to bulldoze the remains back and forth, again and again.

This man and his father were farmers, and for most of their lives they had worked together in the fields. They didn't verbalize much together nor share their feelings. But theirs was a close nonverbal relationship.

You and I may grieve with tears. He grieved with his borrowed bulldozer. This was his personal expression of words and tears. He cried by working the land over and over again until nothing was visible. He gave his father and the family home a proper burial in his own way. The land, which in a sense was his father's cemetery, was now ready to be farmed, and it would be—by the son.

If you were to ask this man why he had done this, he couldn't give you an answer. He didn't know why he had acted out his grief in this way, but he had done something with his grief, and it was probably the best thing he could have done.

The more immobilized you are by your grief, the more dependent and helpless you feel. Doing something—anything—is a healthy step whether it makes sense to anyone else or not. It helps you regain control again.

4. *Be aware that guilt may become your unwelcome companion.* Sometimes guilt causes us to respond in a variety of ways we wouldn't normally respond, from rationalizing and blaming to self-punishment or attempts at atonement. Guilt may try to consume you.

Let me tell you about Sarah. She was rich. Very, very rich. Not only was her income a thousand dollars a day, but she had also inherited 20 million dollars. That's not bad…especially in the late 1800s. By today's standards, she could have been a billionaire. She was well known in society. Just mention her name, and everyone nodded. She was invited to every social event or party. And she had power. Her name opened doors and opportunities. She was sought after by boards, lenders, and politicians. They wanted her support and money.

Sarah had it all…including misery. Her only child had died at five weeks, and then her husband had died. Two losses and two potential crises. She was alone. She had her name, her memories, and her money. There was something else she had as well—quiet. To get away she moved from Connecticut to San Jose, California.

She purchased an eight-room farmhouse as well as the adjoining 160 acres. But then a strange thing happened. She hired 16 carpenters to work on her house, 24 hours a day, every day for the next 38 years. The layout of the house, to put it in today's vernacular, was weird. Each window had 13 panes, each wall 13 panels, each closet 13 hooks, and each chandelier 13 globes.

The floor plan was bizarre. Corridors were put in at random. Some led nowhere. A set of stairs led to a ceiling that had no door, and one door opened to a blank wall. There were tunnels, trap-doors, and secret passageways. The work on this mysterious mansion finally came to a halt when Sarah died. But can you imagine what this house was like after 38 years? It covered six acres and had the following features: 6 kitchens, 13 bathrooms, 40 stairways, 47 fireplaces, 52 skylights, 467 doors, 10,000 windows, 160 rooms, and 1 bell tower.

What would drive a wealthy woman to become so eccentric, so driven, so compulsive? After all, she didn't need what she built. She lived alone. Or did she? A legend evolved that Sarah Winchester had "visitors" every night. The story goes that a servant would go to the bell tower at night via a secret passage and ring the bell. Sarah would then go into the "blue room," which was reserved for her and her guests and stay there until 2:00 A.M. Then the bell would once again ring and the visitors would depart, and Sarah Winchester would go to her room.

The visitors? They were United States soldiers killed on the American frontier. They were slain Indians torn apart by the bullets that struck them. Both soldiers and Indians were killed by that new invention, the repeating Winchester rifle. It brought millions of dollars to the Winchester family, but death to thousands of others. It also brought haunting experiences to Sarah Winchester prompted by guilt that went unresolved. To atone for what had occurred, she tried to provide a home for the dead.[8]

Isn't it interesting how we tend to hook into guilt and end up pointing the finger back at ourselves? Self-blame is usually unrealistic and harsher than the blame we place on others. Our imagination takes the event and magnifies our sense of responsibility. We tell ourselves things like, "If only…" or "I should have…" Listen to some of the statements common to self-blame:

"If only I hadn't allowed him to buy that motorcycle. If only I'd insisted he wear his helmet, he wouldn't be paralyzed now. I should have been home that night. If I'd been there, the accident wouldn't have happened."

"I kick myself all over for not telling Mom I loved her. She's not here now, and I can't let her know. The opportunity is gone forever."

"If I hadn't spent so much time at work, she wouldn't have left me. I was just trying to provide, but I guess I blew it. I kick myself again and again."

"I should have noticed his depression. I just didn't believe what he was saying, and now he's dead—by his own hand."

"Where did we go wrong with that child? I guess we were too young and too ignorant. We blew it, and she's in trouble because of us."

Let's summarize what happens during the impact phase of a crisis. During this phase you will want to face the situation and fight. Or you'll want to flee; you will think in a somewhat numb and disoriented fashion; you will search for whatever it is you have lost, often by reminiscing; you will need people to accept your feelings.

The Withdrawal-Confusion Phase

After the impact phase you're going to move into the withdrawal-confusion phase. This will last for days or even weeks or months depending on the severity of the loss, and you will feel emotionally drained. You are worn out. Remember, the various phases overlap one another and you may move between different phases. That too is normal.

During the withdrawal-confusion phase the tendency to deny your feelings is probably stronger than at any other time. One reason is your feelings now can become the ugliest and most potent. As one emotion triggers another, you may feel intense anger at whatever has occurred, which in some cases brings on guilt for having such feelings. Then you feel shame. The pain from these varied responses increases your desire to repress them. If some of your feelings shock others, you may want to repress them even more.

Expect your feelings to run wild. This is a normal response. In fact, you will probably feel a sense of

- bewilderment: "I never felt this way before."

- danger: "I feel so scared. Something terrible is going to happen."

- confusion: "I can't think clearly. My mind doesn't seem to work."

- impasse: "I'm stuck. Nothing I do seems to help."

- desperation: "I've got to do something, but I don't know what to do."

- apathy: "Nothing can help me. What's the use of trying?"

- helplessness: "I can't cope by myself. Please help me."

- urgency: "I need help *now*."

- discomfort: "I feel so miserable and unhappy."

During the withdrawal-confusion phase your thinking patterns will reflect a certain amount of uncertainty and ambiguity. You just aren't sure what to think or do. You won't think clearly since the thinking part of your brain has taken a hit. Your rationality at this time is overwhelmed by your emotions. And sometimes it will be difficult to identify the feelings and emotions that are churning around inside of you.

During this second phase, you will alternate between bargaining and detachment. Bargaining involves wishful thinking: "If only this hadn't happened," "If only I could recapture what I had," "Perhaps there's some way to bring back what I lost."

In time this type of thinking moves to the detachment level. You will need to detach yourself from whatever it is you've lost, whether it's a job, a friend, or a spouse. A widower cannot stay married to a deceased wife. An expelled student can no longer be a student in the school from which he was expelled. A worker cannot fulfill a job he or she has lost. You distance yourself by saying, "It wasn't that important," "I can do better now that he or she isn't in my life anymore," "I wanted a new job anyway." You do this to ease the pain of your loss. You will need to say goodbye to whatever you lost.

You may find yourself vacillating between performing some routine tasks that need to be done and then reflecting and reminiscing upon how things used to be. You may feel anger at having to give up what you lost, whether it's a person, an object, or an identity. Our natural tendency is to protect ourselves from the emptiness that loss brings. In our attempt to restore what is gone, we tend to distort and glorify the past. We do this to help us face the future. As we reach out to new tasks and even to new people, we do it in an attempt to fill the void in our lives.

During this time you need the assistance of caring friends and relatives to help you organize your life. You'll probably need help in planning your day, arranging appointments, keeping the house or job in order, and so on. Don't be hard on yourself for this apparent defect in your life. It's a normal transition through your grief. And if this is loss of a spouse, it's not time to be looking for another partner. It's time to adjust to the loss. And be careful. This is a time when some people tend to become careless—they get traffic tickets or even have an accident.

Secondary Wounding

There is one additional source of pain you'll need to contend with—other people who make statements that hurt rather than console, hinder rather than comfort, and prolong your pain rather than relieve it. These people are secondary wounders. They will give you unwanted and bad advice as well as improperly applied Scripture. You won't be the first to experience this. Remember Job?

> [Job] had four well-meaning but insufferable friends who came over to cheer him up and try to explain [his suffering]. They said that anybody with enough sense to come in out of the rain knew that God was just. They said that anybody old enough to spell his own name knew that since God was just, he made bad things happen to bad people and good things happen to good people. They said that such being the case, you didn't need a Harvard diploma to figure out that since bad things had happened to Job, then *ipso facto* he must have done something bad himself. But Job hadn't, and he said so, and that's not all he said either. "Worthless physicians are you all," he said. "Oh that you would keep silent, and it would be your wisdom" (Job 13:4-5 RSV). They were a bunch

of theological quacks, in other words, and the smartest thing they could do was shut up. But they were too busy explaining things to listen.[9]

Expect to hear statements you'd rather not hear. It's difficult to respond to these people the way we'd like to because of our traumatized state. Perhaps they'd learn not to make such insensitive statements if someone spoke up and said, "That's not true, and it's not helpful. If you want to be supportive, I would appreciate it if you would..." Sometimes we excuse what these people say as well-meaning, which is questionable. Sometimes they're just reflecting their own anxiety, their fear, and their lack of having dealt with issues in their own lives. Remember, this is not advice coming from experts.

Consider some typical clichés we hear from others when we go through a crisis.

"Be Strong" Clichés

- Big boys don't cry.
- The children are flexible...they will bounce back.
- You must be strong for the children.
- Support groups are for wimps.
- You've just got to get hold of yourself!
- Others have held up well. You can, too.
- Cheer up.
- No sense in crying over spilt milk.
- This is nature's way.

"Hurry Up" Clichés

- You're not your old self.
- Out of sight, out of mind.

- Time will heal.
- You're young, and you'll be able to make a new life for yourself.
- I just don't understand your behavior.
- Life goes on.
- No sense in dwelling on the past.

"Guilt" Clichés

- If you look around, you can always find someone who is worse off than you.
- This is the work of the devil (meaning that if you had a closer relationship with God, the devil couldn't have had his way).
- If I were you, I'd do it this way.
- Count your blessings.
- Only the good die young.
- If you had been a better Christian, this wouldn't have happened to you.
- Think of all your precious memories.
- It's a blessing.

"God" Clichés

- God needs him more than you do.
- He's happy now because he's with God.
- God did this to show how powerful He can be in your life.
- It was God's will.
- God never gives us more than we can handle.
- God helps those who help themselves.

"Discounting" Clichés

- I know just how you feel.
- Silence is golden.
- If there's anything I can do, just call me.
- You can have more children.
- It's better to have loved and lost than never to have loved at all.
- Be glad you don't have problems like mine.
- What you don't know won't hurt you.[10]

Those who share with you in this manner need to be avoided or educated! During this second phase, when the numbness wears off, you begin to feel the pain of hearing comments such as these.

To summarize, in the withdrawal-confusion phase (which will last for days, sometimes for weeks or longer), your response will be emotional. You may feel anger, fear, guilt, even rage. Your thinking process is muddled. You'll vacillate from bargaining to detaching yourself from the lost person or situation.

During this time of puzzled searching for a way out of the difficulty, you need some task-oriented support and help from others. You need friends who will help you make some plans and accomplish small tasks so that you can feel functional. Don't hesitate to let others know that you want to do something or that you need to feel useful.

The Adjustment Phase

The third phase, called the adjustment phase, will take weeks to work through or, with a severe trauma, much longer. But the emotional responses you experience during this time are focused toward hope. Yes, you may feel some depression that comes and goes, but you're starting to form positive attitudes again. You may have positive and negative feelings side by side. You may begin to talk about the future with hope and look forward to enjoying a new job, moving to a new location, rebuilding a fire-destroyed home, considering remarriage. You're looking around for something new to which you can develop an attachment.

Your future dreams or action-steps start to take on special significance. You've been in and through the depths of the valley and now you're climbing up the side of the mountain. Be prepared for the opinions and advice of others. Sift through what you hear.

Others may see no value in what you are doing now. They could question your decisions and actions if what you're doing doesn't jibe with what they think you need to do. Some may feel that you're making a drastic mistake as you take a new step.

Don't make any important decisions during your down times; wait until you feel hope. And don't despair because your feelings fluctuate. Your insight *is* returning. Your objectivity can help you process information and new suggestions.

During this phase, Scripture can assist you in making sound decisions. Now you're more receptive and capable of dealing with spiritual insights than early on in the crisis. Prior to this point, Scripture and prayer resources were there to support and sustain you. But this is the time to seek answers and direction through the teaching and reading of the Word.

The Reconstruction-Reconciliation Phase

The final phase (which can last the longest) is the reconstruction-reconciliation phase. Spontaneous expressions of hope are key elements here. Your sense of confidence has returned, and you can make plans again. You're able to consciously decide not to engage in self-pity anymore.

Initiative, progress, and reattachment are key words during this phase. You've assimilated new places, new activities, new people, new jobs, and new spiritual insight into your life. If your feelings of anger and blame created difficulty during this crisis, now is the time to reconcile with those people you may have offended.

One sign of crisis resolution is the newness of life you feel and the new discoveries you experience. A crisis is an opportunity for you to gain new strengths, new perspectives on life, new appreciation, new values, and a new way to approach the way you live. You'll look at life differently. Hopefully, you won't take it for granted. I know this firsthand.

A number of years ago I experienced some strange physical symptoms. These included vertigo, pressure in the back of my head, and headaches. The symptoms persisted for about seven weeks, during which time the doctors had some theories, but nothing concrete. My own concerns and worries about what this might be added to some of the anxiety I experienced.

Finally, after going through further examinations, including a CAT scan, the symptoms disappeared. As we pieced together what had occurred, we felt the physical symptoms were brought on by my participation in too many strenuous seminars with no recuperation time in between, coupled with a cold and some altitude changes.

Physical exhaustion is one of the greatest culprits of mysterious ailments. But this experience, especially at the age of 47, caused me to think, reevaluate, and consider some changes in my life. I learned to pace my work in a more balanced manner. I learned to play more and to evaluate what was really important to me and what wasn't. I began to say *no.* I didn't necessarily like what I went through, but I grew because of it. After it was over, I felt it had been a necessary experience.

Crises and trials can become the means to exciting growth. I've always been impressed with William Pruitt and his response to a physical problem he conquered. In many ways his crisis was with him for the rest of his life. In his book *Run from the Pale Pony,* Pruitt uses an analogy to describe what happened in his life. In the foreword of the book he writes:

> About thirty years ago, one of my joys as a boy was to ride a white horse named Prince. That proud, spirited stallion carried me where I wanted to go, wherever I bid him to and at the pace which I chose. I don't have to explain to horsemen the feeling of strength, even authority, which comes from controlling such a powerful animal. Nor need I expand upon the excitement I felt when I galloped him at full speed, or about the quiet pride that came when I twisted him through the corkscrew turns of a rodeo exercise. After all, he was mine and I trained him. Those experiences are a part of my heritage.
>
> My cherished white horse was gone and seldom remembered about fifteen years later. It was then that I encountered a completely different kind of horse. When I first became aware of the specter, its shape was too dim to discern. I know only that I had never seen anything like it before. Too, I know that I had not sought any such creature, yet something different was with me wherever I went and that shadow would not go away. No matter what I did, though, the specter followed my every move. Furthermore, the harder I tried to lose it, the clearer the creature's form became to me.
>
> My uneasiness changed to anxiety when I realized that this unwanted shadow had a will of its own. The chill of fear came when

I understood that it had no intention of leaving me alone. Without further warning, it began to communicate with me openly one day, and in a harsh voice which was almost rigid with animosity, it spat out, "You can no longer go where you want to go when you choose at the speed you pick. That's true because I will give you weakness instead of strength. Excitement and pride? Never again will you have them like before. I plan only confinement and disability for you. And I will be your constant companion. My name is Chronic Illness."

At the time I heard it speak, I shrank back from actually seeing it face to face. It spoke harshly of miseries which were inverse to joys with my white horse named Health and the bitter irony was reflected in the form of a malicious creature. Chronic Illness took the shape of a stunted, misshapen pony. Its shaggy coat was pale in color, streaked with ages-old accumulation of dark despair. But, unquestionably, the most frightening feature of the animal was its overwhelming glare, its glare-eyed stare which held me helpless. The pony's wild eyes stared restlessly from side to side, yet strangely were unbinding. This book is written first of all for those people who have met the pale pony face to face.[11]

The "pale pony" might come in many possible forms—serious physical or mental illness, accident, war, or other injuries. Whatever shape the pony takes, the results can be quite similar. William Pruitt's pale pony was multiple sclerosis. He sensed that the disease was increasingly affecting his life, but his story is the story of hope. He realized that he had a number of years before he would be completely disabled, and realizing that he wouldn't be able to carry on the type of work he was in, he went back to college in a wheelchair. He earned a Ph.D. in economics and began to teach on a college level.

Pruitt's book is not about giving up; rather it is about fighting back and *winning*. It is a very honest book, telling of the pain and the hurt and the turmoil. But its emphasis is on faith and hope.

After your crisis, you may not be able to do what you used to do; your life might not return to the way it was. A "normal life" takes on new meaning. But you can look for alternatives. You can discover new ways of responding. You can learn to say, "I will be able to *discover* 'plan B.' There is a different way to live my life!"

When you find yourself (or someone else) experiencing a crisis, look at the "Normal Crisis Pattern" chart on the next page. In fact, make a photocopy, and keep it handy for personal use or to help others when they are in need (perhaps in your Bible). This chart will help remind you that your feelings are normal, and there is hope and light at the end of the tunnel.

Remember, too, that a crisis is an opportunity! It's a time for change and growth. There is one factor—attitude—that causes a major crisis to become a growth-producing experience instead of a restrictive, crippling, eternal tragedy. Our world is unstable; it rocks our boat. We are unstable; we rock our boat. But if our attitude has been built upon the teachings of the Word of God, then we have hope in the midst of an upset world! Isaiah 33:6 says, "And He will be the stability of your times."

Our stability comes from allowing Jesus Christ to be our rock at all times.

The Normal Crisis and Sudden Loss Pattern

	Phase I Impact	Phase II Withdrawal/ Confusion	Phase III Adjustment	Phase IV Reconstruction/ Reconciliation
Time	A few hours to a day	Days to weeks	Weeks to months	Months
Response	Should I stay and face it or withdraw?	Intense emotions. You feel drained, anger, sadness, fear, anxiety, depression, rage, guilt.	Your positive thoughts begin returning along with other emotions.	Hope has returned. Self-confidence builds.
Thoughts	Numb, disoriented. Insight ability limited. Feelings overwhelm.	Thinking ability limited. Uncertainty and ambiguity. Problem solving not working.	You're now able to problem solve.	Thinking is clearer. Encouraged by ability to solve problems.
Direction you take to regain control	You search for what you lost. Denial. What worked before?	Bargaining-wishful-thinking. Detachment.	You begin looking for something new to invest in.	Progress is evident and new attachments are made to something significant.
Searching behavior	Often reminiscing.	Puzzled, unclear.	You can now stay focused and begin to learn from your experience.	You may want to stop and evaluate where you've been and where you're going.

4

"Why Do I Feel This Way?"

Reading the Message in Painful Emotions

They hit with the intensity of a tornado and the suddenness of an earthquake. They won't go away when you want them to, and there's no way to evict them. They're like a runaway train whose brakes have burned out. You feel totally out of control. Even though you may question the necessity of their presence, they do have a purpose. What do we call these "unfriendly" companions? *Emotions. Feelings.*

During a crisis, you may experience many kinds of emotions, and perhaps some feelings you've never felt before. It's not just the presence of the emotions that bothers you, it's their intensity.

When you understand that feeling an emotion is an unavoidable human condition, and you know what to expect from emotions, you will handle them better. Many people feel they alone experience such intense feelings. This misbelief keeps them from accepting their feelings, learning from them, and moving on to recovery. Which emotions are your most frequent companions?

Anger

Anger is a sign of protest. It's a natural and predictable emotion during a crisis or after a loss. It's a reaction against something that shouldn't have happened. It's a way of fighting back when you feel helpless. Your perception of the way things are, or the way they should be, has been altered. Your belief system has been damaged. Anger is a normal reaction when you are deprived of something you value.

Expressions of anger against the injustices of life have always been with us. In the Bible, we find anger expressed in the psalms and the books of the prophets. Job expressed anger at God, as did Jonah and Elijah.

Hundreds of years ago the American Indians shot arrows into the air to drive away evil spirits. We still do this, but we do it in a different way. We shake our fists, we verbalize, we write letters, and in some cases, we file lawsuits.

Sometimes we run into problems with anger. Society doesn't always know how to respond to our anger, and neither do many people in the church. That's because they often have an incorrect perspective of Scripture on this subject, and they attempt to project that perspective on others.

Let's take a look at some of the typical ways we direct our anger to avoid dealing with our pain.

Anger at God

Too often there is no appropriate object on which to vent our anger, so we begin looking for anything! Whom do we get angry at most often? God. We blame Him—He shouldn't have done this, or He shouldn't have allowed that. He's supposed to do things right—the way we want it!

When we blame God, we can unnerve and unsettle other people. They may respond with Christian clichés or try to convince us that our anger at God is irrational. They fail to realize that nothing they say will help, because we are living on emotions at this point. Even though we may be raising questions, we're not really looking for answers.

People who recover successfully from a crisis vent their anger rather than stuff it. They realize that to deny anger buries it alive, and someday there will be a resurrection. Buried anger can lead to addiction, alcohol abuse, and depression. It can blow up on others or blow in on ourselves with depression or other self-destructive behavior. But when anger is expressed to God it can be analyzed, dealt with, and can lead to a rediscovery of the character and purposes of God.

Anger at the Unfairness of Life

You may be angry at the unfairness of the world—the unfairness of life itself. In 1995 in Los Angeles, a garbage truck pulled alongside a school bus loaded with children. A part of the apparatus malfunctioned and a large steel beam shot through the window of the bus, killing two young students instantly. Why them? Why so young? Why not the irresponsible ones? We raise these questions in vain. Because they are unanswerable, anger, disillusionment, and even irrationality become part of our emotional state.

After the crash of TWA Flight 800 into the waters off Long Island, New York, there was an outburst of anger on many fronts. That day a small town in Pennsylvania lost several high school students and chaperons on their way to France for two weeks of study. Even one death in a small community is felt by almost everyone, but when several are killed, the whole community plunges into crisis. The unfairness of losing so many from a small area generates an outburst against the unfairness of the world. The loss of the men and women working in the World Trade Center and the rescue workers was a crushing experience. Our country was put into shock and grief.

Anger at Others

Our anger may also be directed at other people. Family members of those killed on TWA Flight 800 were angry because victims were recovered slowly, and because details were announced from the media rather than the proper authorities. They were angry at TWA, the media, the recovery workers, and the politicians.

There was a smoldering anger in our nation against those who perpetrated the devastation in Oklahoma City in 1995 and New York City in 2001. There was visible anger at the terrorists and with the countries who harbored such people.

We even get angry at those who haven't had to experience what we've gone through. Because they haven't experienced, or we think they haven't experienced, the devastation that we have, part of us wants them to have to suffer what we've suffered. It's unfair—why should they be let off the hook?

Because we believe the tragedy or crisis shouldn't have happened, we look for something or someone to blame—a doctor, a hospital, an organization, a CEO, an accountant, a bus driver, or anyone we perceive as having somehow participated in the crisis. Sometimes our anger is vented toward anyone who is around, especially family members.

The bereaved get angry at the physician who tried in vain to help a loved one. Fire and flood victims get angry at the police and firefighters who were unable to save their homes. Widows often feel anger toward close family members after the first few weeks of bereavement. They feel overprotected, and overcontrolled, or they feel unsupported and disappointed because they expected assistance from others.

We're angry at terrorists and nations who harbor terrorists, and we *should* be angry.

You may get angry at those who fail to reach out and support you during your time of trouble. When we hurt, we want to be acknowledged. We don't want people to pretend that everything is okay. It isn't. In some cases it never will be the same. Of course, part of the reason we end up feeling isolated is because no one has taught us how to minister to each other during a time of need. Fortunately, this is starting to change.

Sometimes, if your crisis was the death of a loved one, you may feel anger at the one who died. Survivors sometimes feel deserted or victimized. The loss of a spouse or a parent may leave you with the responsibility of what they left undone. Often anger comes because we feel out of control, powerless, and victimized.

Anger at Self

You may direct your anger inward. Women are more likely to do this, while men generally turn anger outward. Anger turned inward is quite common after physical loss as well as when one is the victim of a crime. Intense self-directed anger can be immobilizing.

How do you deal with anger in a positive way? You admit it, you accept it, and you release it in a healthy way. You use anger's energy to do something constructive. Mothers Against Drunk Drivers (MADD) was founded because of the constructive use of anger directed toward a major problem in our society—drinking and driving. The MADD organization has made society aware of the problem of drunk drivers on our roads and highways and has helped to establish and reinforce laws to prosecute those who victimize others through their negligence. There are other examples of anger directed to constructive ends.

A family who lost their son in a swimming accident at a lake organized a group of parents to convince resort managers and fish and game officials to post warning signs about water hazards to help prevent other similar tragedies.

A young mother whose two-year-old died in the cancer ward of a hospital developed a cooperative program among 15 churches in her city to set up support groups for parents of young children who have died. In addition, each church solicited huge toy donations from merchants and families for the hospital pediatric ward.

Actress Theresa Saldano almost lost her life in a premeditated violent attack. She was stabbed again and again, and required more than a thousand stitches in her body. The attack left her with feelings of terror, intense pain, and rage. In her book *Beyond Survival* she said it was her rage that gave her the energy to fight pain, death, and the sick desires of her assailant. It was also her rage at society's treatment of victims that gave her the vision to form a victim advocacy group called "Victims for Victims."

I don't know if anger over the accident that paralyzed him is what prompted Christopher Reeve to accomplish what he has. But he's worked hard to gain financial support, increase public and government awareness, and lobby for new legislation to help victims of spinal cord damage. He has written each United States senator personally, and has helped to raise millions of dollars for research on this problem.[1]

Perhaps you could write a letter (don't mail it!) to whomever you're angry at and then sit in a room and read it aloud. During my counseling sessions in New York after the World Trade Center disaster, I had numerous people write an angry letter to the terrorists. Many people have found release by journaling each day to release pent-up feelings of anger. The point is, those who move ahead come to grips with their anger in constructive ways.

A friend of mine, Jessica Shaver, wrote the following poem that depicts what so many people have discovered.

I Told God I Was Angry

I told God I was angry.
I thought He'd be surprised.
I thought I'd kept hostility
quite cleverly disguised.

I told the Lord I hate Him.
I told Him that I hurt.
I told Him that He isn't fair,
He's treated me like dirt.

I told God I was angry
but *I'm* the one surprised.
"What I've known all along," He said,
"you've finally realized.

"At last you have admitted
what's really in your heart.
Dishonesty, not anger,
was keeping us apart.

"Even when you hate Me
I don't stop loving you.
Before you can receive that love
you must confess what's true.

"In telling Me the anger
you genuinely feel,
it loses power over you,
permitting you to heal."

I told God I was sorry
And He's forgiven me.
The truth that I was angry
has finally set me free.

Guilt

Another companion of crisis is guilt. This is a normal response and can often be traced to our tendency to place blame, but now we end up pointing the finger back at ourselves.

Guilt is present in any crisis when we feel that we've fallen short in some way or have violated something we believe in. However, often the standards we set for ourselves are based upon unrealistic and inappropriate expectations.

Crisis brought on by the loss of another person, whether it's through a broken relationship, divorce, or death, often moves us into a selective memory mode. That is, we tend to remember everything that was negative in our relationship while failing to recall the positive. Initially in this type of loss we tend to dwell on the negative things we contributed to the relationship and overstate the good things the other person contributed.

Guilt grows when we repeat the "if onlys," "could haves," "should haves," and "shouldn't haves." I've heard statements like "I should have known CPR," "I shouldn't have let him ride that motorcycle," or "If only I'd had the radio on, I would have heard the tornado warning."

This type of reaction is especially true when the loss involves a child. For example, after the crisis of a miscarriage or stillbirth, parents question themselves and each other. They wonder if it happened because of something they did or didn't do.

When an adolescent chooses a different lifestyle or value system, a parent asks, "Where did I go wrong?" "Why didn't I spend more time with him?" "Why didn't I take an interest in his schoolwork?" "If only I had homeschooled him instead."

We may even feel guilty over some of the feelings we experience during the upset of a crisis. I've talked to many people who have said their guilt came because during a crisis, they doubted God, questioned God, didn't have enough faith, didn't believe enough, or weren't spiritual enough. When guilt enters our life, whether it's realistic or exaggerated, we tend to develop an unhealthy preoccupation with how bad we are. We look at ourselves in a distorted way. We focus on our sinful state and fail to remember God's offer of forgiveness.

More and more today we hear about survivor guilt. Accidents, tornadoes, earthquakes, and terrorist attacks create a special kind of remorse in those who survive the tragic event. There were many survivors of the Oklahoma City bombing with only minor injuries or no injuries at all. Many of them experienced survival guilt. The firemen and police officers who survived the collapse of the Trade Towers in New York talk about their sense of guilt in escaping death. There were those who didn't go to work that day or left early or went downstairs and missed the collapse of the towers. They too ask, "Why me?" but for a different reason. Even some of the family members of those who were lost in TWA Flight 800 ended up asking, "Why them? It should have been me. They were too young. I'm older." This type of questioning often happens when the tragedy affects a well-known person or a child. The belief that it would have been more sensible for the tragedy to have happened to you rather than the other person is a clear indication of survivor guilt. At the heart of these feelings could be the belief that you were allowed to avoid the tragedy at the cost of the other person. That feeling is rarely anchored in fact.

Two Kinds of Guilt

There are two kinds of guilt. Some call them good guilt and bad guilt, others call them legitimate guilt and illegitimate guilt. Guilt that is often out of proportion to an event is the bad or illegitimate kind of guilt. Feeling this kind of guilt can be normal in a crisis that involves the loss of a significant person, and usually it comes from the unrealistic beliefs we hold, the "I should haves" that no one could ever attain.

The person who moves on in life from a crisis talks over his or her feelings with a person holding an objective outlook on the situation. If the only one you're talking to about your guilt is yourself, then remember, you are biased. A nonjudgmental person can help you look at whatever is creating your guilt feelings, whether they be acts, thoughts, or some perceived omissions. Another person's rationality can help you evaluate your guilt and keep you from overemphasizing the negative.[2]

As you do this, you'll find your guilt diminishing over a period of time. And when the guilt creeps in, you're able to evict it more quickly each time it occurs. Whenever guilt becomes a part of your life, the following questions may help you evaluate it. You may find help by discussing these questions with a trusted friend.

- What is the reason for the guilt I feel? Is there something I did or didn't do? If so, what was it? Would anyone else agree that I was truly responsible?

- Is what I did wrong or contrary to God's Word and teaching in any way?

- Is this something I need to make restitution for or confess to anyone?

There may be legitimate, or good, guilt in your life. Good guilt has a purpose: It shows us where we've gone wrong and what we need to change. It can motivate us to grow. This legitimate guilt (which you could experience in a crisis) happens where there is a direct cause-and-effect relationship. When this kind of guilt happens, we can do something about it. We can admit what we've done, make restitution if necessary, and above all confess it and receive God's forgiveness. Scripture shows us the feelings of a man struggling with real guilt in Psalm 51:1-12:

> Be gracious to me, O God, according to Your
> lovingkindness;
> According to the greatness of Your compassion blot out my transgressions.
> Wash me thoroughly from my iniquity
> And cleanse me from my sin.
> For I know my transgressions,
> And my sin is ever before me.
> Against You, You only, I have sinned
> And done what is evil in Thy sight,
> So that You art justified when You speak,
> And blameless when Thou dost judge.
>
> Behold, I was brought forth in iniquity
> And in sin my mother conceived me.
> Behold, You desire truth in the innermost
> being,
> And in the hidden part You will make me
> know wisdom.
> Purify me with hyssop, and I shall be clean;
> Wash me, and I shall be whiter than snow.
> Make me to hear joy and gladness,
> Let the bones which You have broken
> rejoice.
> Hide Your face from my sins,
> And blot out all my iniquities.
>
> Create in me a clean heart, O God,
> And renew a steadfast spirit within me.
> Do not cast me away from Your presence,
> And do not take Your Holy Spirit from me.

Restore to me the joy of Your salvation,
And sustain me with a willing spirit.

Forgiveness belongs to us. It is always there. It can't be bought; we can't work for it. It's a gift.

I acknowledged my sin to You,
And my iniquity I did not hide;
I said, "I will confess my transgressions to the
    LORD";
And You forgave the guilt of my sin.

PSALM 32:5

If we confess our sins, He is faithful and righteous to forgive us our sins and to cleanse us from all unrighteousness.

1 JOHN 1:9

One of the most graphic passages about guilt is in the *Living Bible:*

There was a time when I wouldn't admit what a sinner I was. But my dishonesty made me miserable and filled my days with frustration. All day and all night your hand was heavy on me. My strength evaporated like water on a sunny day until I finally admitted all my sin to you and stopped trying to hide them. I said to myself, "I will confess them to the Lord." And you forgave me! All my guilt is gone.

PSALMS 32:3-5 TLB

Perhaps what one person wrote can encourage us to deal with our guilt.

If only I had...

treated the one I loved
more kindly.

called the doctor sooner.

understood the full extent
of the illness.

taken better care of
him or her.

not lost my temper.

expressed my affection
more frequently.

When death comes, life is
examined.

You become acutely aware of your failures,
real or imagined.
You want to rectify past errors.
You wish to compensate for
the wrongs you have committed.
Some people even punish themselves
with self-destructive acts,

as if to say: "See how much I am suffering. Doesn't this
prove my great love?"
Self-recrimination becomes a way
to undo all the things that
make you now feel guilty.

And maybe you were guilty.
Perhaps you said things you
should not have said.
Perhaps you neglected to do things
you should have done.
But who hasn't?

What is past is past.
It cannot be changed.

You already have too much pain
to add to the burden of self-
accusation, self-reproach, and
self-depreciation.[3]

Fear

One of the most common emotions we experience in a
crisis is fear. Perhaps what fear does to us is best described
by the following passages from God's Word.

I heard and my inward parts trembled,
At the sound my lips quivered.
Decay enters my bones,
And in my place I tremble.
Because I must wait quietly for the day of
distress,
For the people to arise who will invade us.

Habakkuk 3:16

Anxiety in a man's heart weighs it down,
But a good word makes it glad.

Proverbs 12:25

All the days of the desponding and afflicted
are made evil [by anxious thoughts and fore-
bodings], but he who has a glad heart has a
continual feast [regardless of circumstances].

Proverbs 15:15 AMP

The word *fear* comes from the Old English word *faer*,
which means "sudden calamity or danger." The Hebrew
word for fear can mean "dread."

Usually we can identify the source of our fears or "dreads." Anxiety, however, is fear with a high level of apprehension that's not directly related to anything specific. It can be very disturbing to experience these anxious feelings without knowing why. The anxiety or fear can cause numerous symptoms such as rapid heartbeat, ringing in the ears, loss of appetite, upset stomach, nausea, dizziness, nightmares, tightening of the throat and difficulty in swallowing, muscle pain, poor concentration, memory lapses, sweaty palms, and difficulty sleeping. There isn't a part of our bodies that can't be affected by anxiety.

Fear often brings along its close companion—worry. Worry is an uneasy, suffocating feeling that covers everything we see with a cloud of pessimism. It stirs up our minds and churns our stomachs. The root meaning of the word is "to choke or strangle." It's like racing the engine of a car while it's in neutral. Worry immobilizes us and causes us to focus on the worst possible outcome. We ask "What if?" again and again, each time making our answer a bit worse.

Worry is like fog. Perhaps you've driven in a dense fog that completely hid anything more than a few feet from your car. Fog has the ability to snarl the traffic of a major city and shut down an international airport. Yet a dense fog that covers seven city blocks to a depth of one hundred feet is composed of less than one glass of water.

In a similar way, a little bit of worry can fog up a lot of reality. It chills your outlook and makes everything look hazy, including your perception of life. It's so easy to fall into a pattern of worry. If that's where you are right now, you're not alone.

Your feelings of anxiety are normal. You're not going crazy. Although you want to know why you're experiencing these disturbing, anxious feelings and thoughts, you may not know for quite a while. Most likely you fear that the crisis that has shattered your expectations—your beliefs and your world—could happen again. For instance, the fear of "when and where and how will terrorists strike our country again?" has recently become a part of our national life. The more sudden and intense the crisis event, the more fear and anxiety you may experience as a result. It will help to keep in mind that you can't always explain why you feel the way you do. Also, your fear and anxiety will not always be with you. Help is available, and you will get relief.

Responding Rightly to Fear

Survivors are those who confront their fears, identify them, put them in perspective, and allow them to diminish slowly while they focus on positive improvement. Many survivors have found it helpful to list each of their fears and place a check by it each time it occurs. It also helps to identify what you used to fear and how you overcame it.

There's nothing that helps one to overcome fear as much as concentrating upon God's Word and committing it to memory. God can use passages such as Isaiah 41:10; 43:1; Philippians 4:6-9; and Psalm 37:1-10 to bring you the peace you are looking for. Never avoid or give in to your fears, since each time you do so, fear grows. Face fear, admit you're fearful, and then evict it.

Years ago I was privileged to meet a pastor's wife, the author of an inspiring article about a letter she wrote to her children. The letter expressed how she was struggling with a reocurrence of cancer. In one part of the letter she talked about fear:

> Fear has knocked at my door. Sometimes in the past five days I have let fear in for awhile. It has not been good. I have thought of silly things like: I can't wear that new spring suit we just bought on sale or that lovely wool

skirt we've waited six months for. Other times I think how much I want to see Kathy graduate, go off to Bible school, fall in love with the finest Christian man this world has ever seen, and then watch her walk down the aisle on her dad's arm. Then I think I want to see Kim married and settled. Finally, for sure, I would like grandchildren.

But, dear children of mine, these are human thoughts, and to dwell on them is not healthy. I know one of the strongest desires God has given us is the desire to live, but I want to say to God that I trust Him in this too. My vision is so limited. These human desires are the purest on earth, but if I had even a tiny glimpse of heaven I wouldn't want to stay here. Because I am human, I do. So I have decided that I will put a "No Trespassing" sign at the entrance of the path of human desires and not let my thoughts wander down it.

When fear knocks, it is my determined choice to let faith answer the door, faith that is settled on the sure promise of the Word of God.[4]

How can you accomplish this kind of settled decision? Sometimes it means asking others for help. Your fear could have a useful component to it. It could prompt you to make some necessary changes. It could be that some of your fears have value!

A conversation I recently overheard between a man and woman illustrates the healthy respect we need to have for useful fears. This couple was discussing a life-threatening experience they faced. The man asked, "Aren't you afraid?" The woman's response was tinged with anger:

Of course, I'm afraid! What kind of person do you think I am? It isn't sensible not to be afraid when there is good reason for it. I was afraid when I was beaten as a child. I was afraid when my husband left me. I've spent a lot of my life being afraid. Show me someone who hasn't! That's why so many people resort to drugs and alcohol. It blots out their fear. There is nothing so outstanding about having fear as long as you don't act fearful—because of your fear. We've got to face our fear and move ahead.

Depression

When your crisis involves a major loss or disruption of your life, depression, the "common cold of the mind," begins to take over. It's to be expected. When hope is gone and the future looks bleak, despair finds fertile soil in your mind.

Losses are often at the heart of depression. Any loss can trigger a reactive depression—the loss of a person, a job, a home, a car, a valued photograph, a pet. The stronger the attachment, the more intense the feelings of loss. Loss is especially devastating for women because they put so much of themselves into relationships and build such strong attachments. Especially devastating is the loss of a love relationship. Maggie Scarf describes this dilemma in her classic book *Unfinished Business:*

It is around losses of love that the clouds of despair tend to converge, hover, and darken. Important figures leaving or dying; the inability to establish another meaningful bond with a peer-partner, being forced, by a natural transition in life, to relinquish an important love tie; a marriage that is ruptured, threatening to rupture, or simply growing progressively distant; the splintering of a love affair or recognition that it is souring and will come to nothing.[5]

Often these losses lead to a crisis, but too frequently loss is not recognized as such. We're not made aware of how losses can affect us.

The Old Testament story of Job illustrates in detail the role loss plays in bringing on depression. Job experienced loss to a greater degree than most of us will ever experience. He lost his wealth, his means of livelihood, his servants, and his children. Eventually he lost his own physical health and sense of well-being. He experienced the depths of depression. Listen to his complaints:

Let the day perish wherein I was born,
    and the night which said,
    "A man-child is conceived."
Let that day be darkness!

Why did I not die at birth,
    come forth from the womb and expire?

Why is light given to him that is in misery,
    and life to the bitter in soul,
who long for death, but it comes not,
    and dig for it more than for hid treasures;

For my sighing comes as my bread,
    and my groanings are poured out like water.

In truth I have no help in me,
    and any resource is driven from me.

> So I am allotted months of emptiness,
>> and nights of misery are apportioned to
>> me.
> When I lie down I say, "When shall I arise?"
>> But the night is long,
>> and I am full of tossing till the dawn.
>>> JOB 3:3-4,11,20-21,24;6:13;7:3-4, RSV

No one is immune to depression, not even a Christian. Some people will experience mild depression while others dive to the depths of despondency.

The deeper your depression, the more paralyzing is your sense of helplessness. You feel passive and resigned. Everything seems out of focus. You feel as though you're in a deep, dark pit, cold and isolated. There doesn't seem to be a way out of this pit either. Depression can blind us to the realities of life. It narrows our perception of the world. We end up feeling all alone, as though no one else cares about us.

Depression affects you spiritually and can change the way you see God. It's hard to believe in a loving and personal God who knows the answers and wants us to succeed and yet seems to be far off. The psalmist reflected these feelings as well:

> Lord, be kind to me because I am weak.
>> Heal me, Lord, because my bones ache.
> I am very upset.
>> Lord, how long will it be?
> Lord, return and save me.
>> Save me because of your kindness.
> Dead people don't remember you.
>> Those in the grave don't praise you.
> I am tired of crying to you.
>> Every night my bed is wet with tears.

My bed is soaked from my crying.
My eyes are weak from so much crying.
> They are weak from crying about my
> enemies.

PSALM 6:2-7 NCV

In place of experiencing peace and joy—the light of God in your life—you feel just the opposite. You feel empty. Often Christians who are depressed feel even worse because of their false beliefs about depression. *It is not a sin for a Christian to be depressed.* And most of our depression is not brought on by sin.

Many people are surprised to read the account of Jesus' depression in the Garden of Gethsemane. Jesus was perfect man and free from all sin, yet complete in His humanity and tempted as we are. Look at the account in Matthew 26:36-38 AMP:

> Then Jesus went with them to a place called Gethsemane, and He told His disciples, Sit down here while I go over yonder and pray. And taking with Him Peter and the two sons of Zebedee, He began to show grief and distress of mind and was deeply depressed. Then He said to them, My soul is very sad and deeply grieved, so that I am almost dying of sorrow. Stay here and keep awake and keep watch with Me.

Jesus knew what was about to happen to Him, and it depressed Him. He did not feel guilty over being depressed, and neither should we. But our depression creates a distortion of life and intensifies any guilt feelings we have. Thus, guilt over depression leads to more depression!

If you tend toward depression even before experiencing a crisis, then your depression will be intensified during a crisis.

Learning from Depression

Listen to your depression. There's a message in it. It's telling you that something is amiss in your life. It's like a warning system or a protective device that can keep you from further stress. Admit your feelings to another person who can help you. Don't believe the messages your depression is telling you, for depression heavily distorts reality toward the negative. Be aware that depression immobilizes you and makes you feel lethargic. You actually begin to behave in a way that will reinforce your depression. You will need to counter your feelings and do the opposite of what your feelings tell you. You may be able to do this by yourself, or you may not.

Listen to what Jane learned about her depression:

> I've struggled with this depression for ten months now. My divorce, along with the demotion at work, crushed me. Through counseling and reading I finally got to the place where I could accept my depression as normal, and I didn't feel guilty over it. One day I sat down and tried to figure out what my depression was trying to say to me. It dawned on me that the depression was a symptom, and there were causes. I began to list them. The two losses helped to bring on my depression. So did the fact that I was rejected by my husband and at work. I was eating more to help me feel better, but it made me not like myself. So I made some plans with some friends to hold me accountable. I'm learning to grieve my losses and say good-bye to some dreams. I've learned that since I was rejected I started to reject myself. I'm no longer doing that! And I've changed

my food habits. The depression is still around, but I see it lifting. Now I have the hope that someday it will leave.

If feelings of lethargy and depression have settled over you like a fog, learn as much as you can about depression. Read about it. Discover its meaning for your life. Consider what you have been through recently. Your depression is just a part of the normal array of feelings you may need to experience as you move on to recovery. Above all, keep focused on the strength of the Lord and His Word.

Those who survive are people with faith, especially faith in the promises of God. Dwell on His promises. Believe them:

> Blessed are those who mourn, for they will be comforted.
>
> MATTHEW 5:4

> Come to Me, all who are weary and heavy-laden, and I will give you rest.
>
> MATTHEW 11:28

> Blessed be the God and Father of our Lord Jesus Christ, the Father of mercies and God of all comfort; who comforts us in all our affliction.
>
> 2 CORINTHIANS 1:3-4

> When you pass through the waters, I will be with you; and through the rivers, they will not overflow you. When you walk through the fire, you will not be scorched, nor will the flame burn you.
>
> ISAIAH 43:2

In the same way the Spirit also helps our weakness; for we do not know how to pray as we should, but the Spirit Himself intercedes for us with groanings too deep for words.

ROMANS 8:26

For I am convinced that neither life nor death, nor angels, nor principalities, nor things present, nor things to come, nor powers, nor height, nor depth, nor any other created thing, will be able to separate us from the love of God, which is in Christ Jesus our Lord.

ROMANS 8:38-39

My grace is sufficient for you, for power is perfected in weakness.

2 CORINTHIANS 12:9

For You light my lamp; The LORD my God illuminates my darkness.

PSALM 18:28

The LORD is my light and my salvation; Whom shall I fear? The LORD is the defense of my life; Whom shall I dread?

PSALM 27:1

Perhaps the best way to deal with emotions that invade your life is to follow the example of a hiker who had just read the Forest Service instructions of what to do when encountering wild animals, especially mountain lions. This man was jogging with his dog and came upon a mountain lion. The lion began to stalk the man and then ran after him. Fortunately, the man remembered what he had read. He stopped, turned around, and faced the mountain lion. The lion wasn't expecting this, so it stopped and walked away. Your emotions are like that mountain lion. Face them head-on, listen to their message, and eventually you'll rise above them.

When we go through a crisis, we sometimes believe that God has abandoned us. He hasn't.

When we go through a crisis, we sometimes feel as if nothing matters. There are things that matter.

When we go through a crisis we sometimes think life is not worth living. It is!

In times of loss and sorrow, we people of faith have to "believe against the grain." In our weakness, God reveals His strength, and we can do more than we thought possible.

Faith means clinging to God in spite of our circumstances. It means following Him when we can't see Him. It means being faithful to Him when we don't feel like it.

Resilient people have a creed that says, "I believe!" and they affirm their creed daily. In essence they say:

- I believe God's promises are true.

- I believe heaven is real.

- I believe God will see me through.

- I believe nothing can separate us from God's love.

- I believe God has work for me to do.

"Believing against the grain" means having a survivalist attitude. Not only can we survive a crisis, but out of it we can create something good.[6]

Suggested Reading

Winning Over Your Emotions, H. Norman Wright, Harvest House.

Good Women Get Angry, Dr. Gary Oliver and H. Norman Wright, Servant.

Why Worry? Conquering a Common Inclination, James R. Beck and David T. Moore, Baker.

Dark Clouds, Silver Linings, Dr. Archibald Hart, Focus on the Family.

Coping with Depression, Siang-Yang Tan and John Ortberg, Baker.

"Who Am I Now?"

Adjusting to the Loss of a Family Member

The loss of significant people in our lives is inevitable. We will all face such a loss sometime. Often the loss happens suddenly and traumatically. At other times the loss is expected. Either way, it can be a tremendous crisis and can sometimes bring a significant loss of identity.

Since 1988 I've lost three cousins, two uncles, a sister-in-law, my mother, my mother-in-law, and my son. When the loss is a highly significant person, we feel pain, and nothing and no one can prepare us for the extent of that pain. Has anyone told you what to expect when you lose your parents, a sibling, a child, or a friend? I doubt it. But most of us will experience such a loss. We grieve when a major loss like this occurs. We call it "grief work" because grieving is work.

When you lose a significant person, you will grieve not only over the person you have lost, but also over the wishes, needs, hopes, dreams, and unfulfilled expectations you had for them. You may also grieve not just for your present loss, but also for what you have lost in the future. Perhaps there was something you never had in your relationship with that person, and now you realize you will never have it. I've worked with numerous women who didn't have a good relationship with their father. When he died, that shut the door on any hope they had for reconciliation.

This chapter cannot tell you all you need to know about grieving over the loss of significant people in your life. But it will alert you to concerns and issues that most people have never considered. Knowing this will help give you the resilience you need.

When Your Loss Is Sudden

When you lose a significant person in a sudden, unexpected death, you are at high risk for a pattern of complicated grieving. Those who lost loved ones in the Trade Towers and planes on September 11, 2001 qualify. So do most of the survivors. Sometimes the grief response evolves to a condition known as Post Traumatic Stress Disorder (PTSD), which you will read about in a later chapter. Why does this happen? Consider the cumulative effect of the following factors when your capacity to cope crumbles due to a sudden loss:

- Your assumptions about control, predictability, and security are lost.

- Your loss makes no sense whatsoever.

- It's difficult to recognize the loss.

- You can't even say good-bye or finish any unfinished business.

- Your emotional reactions are heightened much more than when a natural death occurs.

    Your symptoms of grief and shock persist, which demoralizes you.

    You may tend to hold yourself responsible more than you normally would.

    You experience a profound loss of security and confidence in your world. In fact, you're shattered.

    You tend to focus on the negative aspects of the relationship with the deceased, rather than having a balanced view.

    You have sudden major secondary losses because of the unexpectedness of the loss.

All of these factors could lead you to experience PTSD.[1]

As you recover from such a significant crisis or loss, at times you will be ambushed by grief. There's no other way to describe it. Some call it a "grief spasm." It's an ongoing onslaught of grief that hits you suddenly when you least expect it. You may choke up or cry, your chest may feel constricted, and a wave of sadness may overwhelm you. This is a normal response, but when it happens you need to stop everything else and deal with your feelings.[2]

As you grieve, you endeavor to come to the place where you can accept and live with the loss of a significant person in a healthy way.

One of the tasks of grief is learning how to function without this person in your life. You won't have the interactions and validation you were used to experiencing with that person. The loss of their physical presence in your life means that your needs, hopes, dreams, expectations, feelings, and thoughts will change. Slowly, over time, the reality of separation begins to sink in and you realize, "For now, I exist without this person as a part of my life."

When you lose a person, you may discover it will take time to identify all the ways this person was a part of your life. It's a step-by-step process. The loss of his or her companionship, support, judgment—all of these are new and separate losses that make up the loss of your loved one.

Each time you start to respond to the person who is no longer there, you discover again that he or she is gone. It's a fact, and there will be many painful reminders. You may automatically turn to the person to take care of a task he or she usually handled for you only to realize anew that the person is gone.

Whenever someone is gone from your life, you have to *broaden your roles and your skills* and learn to function without the person. You learn to make up for what you have lost. You change what you do, take over new responsibilities, and find other people to help. There may be some things you don't do anymore. Adjustment necessitates not behaving the same way you did when the person was a part of your world. (This is also true when you lose a significant activity in your life through job loss, expulsion from school, loss of a house, and so on).

Moving Beyond Grief

Getting on with your life involves several steps, some of which may come as a surprise to you. Few people are aware of these steps before they experience a major loss.

Some people either resist these steps or become stuck in their grief work. Sometimes after people have gone through these stages they are able to sit down and identify what they have experienced. But what a difference it can make in your life if you're aware of the process at the time you're going through it. The awareness doesn't necessarily lessen the pain, but it gives you a map and lets you know you're on track and not going crazy. These steps apply to the more serious losses.

One of the first things you must do is *develop a new relationship* with the person you lost. You have to untie the ties that connected you to this person. The change involves keeping the loved one alive in your memory in a healthy and appropriate manner.

Formation of a new identity without this person's presence in your life is another step. As one person said, "That portion of my life is history. I'll never be that way or be that person again."

Most couples who marry dream of growing old together. But when the crisis of death occurs, there is not only the loss of that dream but many secondary losses as well. Hopes, wishes, fantasies, feelings, expectations, and the needs that you had for that person are gone.

There's a loss in the future as well. Your identity is now that of a widow or widower, a single person rather than a married one. When a wife loses her husband, she loses someone with whom she would have shared retirement, birthdays, the bed, church functions, children and grandchildren, and weddings. Look at all the roles a spouse fulfills, and what is lost when he or she dies.

friend	parent
handyperson	protector
lover	organizer
gardener	provider
companion	cook
sports partner	bill payer
checkbook balancer	laundry person
mechanic	confidant
encourager	mentor
motivator	prayer partner
business partner	source of inspiration or insight

errand person	teacher
tax preparer	counselor
child	

As you walk through these steps and do your grief work, the emotional energy once invested in the person you lost is now freed up and reinvested in other people, activities, and hopes that in turn can give emotional satisfaction back to you.

Death ends a loved one's life but not your relationship with that person. How do you develop a new relationship with the person you have lost? This isn't a morbid or pathological process. It's a normal response. Yet have you ever heard a discussion about such a relationship? Probably not. If people tell you that the best way to deal with your loss is to forget the person, they're restricting your grief experience.

We keep people alive all the time as we reflect upon who they were, their achievements, and their impact upon us and society. I've heard numbers of people say, "I wonder what he would think if he were alive today," or "Wouldn't she be surprised to see all of this!"

It helps to be with others who have experienced the same type of loss, for they can assist you in the process of adjusting to your new identity.

How Long Will I Feel This Way?

How long does it take to recover and complete your mourning? Much longer than most people believe. The amount of time can vary, depending upon many factors.

It's been said that the average length of mourning is approximately two years for a natural death. In the case of a terminally ill individual, the time following the death could be less, since some of the grieving happened prior to the death.

The unanticipated nature of an accidental death can be a major factor in contributing to a grief reaction that lasts for several years. One study indicated that the majority of mourners who experienced the loss of a spouse or child in an automobile accident were still dealing with the death in thoughts, memories, and feelings four to seven years afterward.[3] It could take longer if you were involved in the same accident.

No one can tell you how long your grief will last. Grief has a beginning, a middle, and an end. But many get stuck in the middle, and most don't understand the dynamics and the duration of grief. This makes it even more difficult to adjust.

The emotional upheaval associated with bereavement includes a number of common elements: a sense of yearning and searching; a sensitivity to stimuli; feelings of anger, guilt, ambiguity, impatience, and restlessness; and a strong need to test what is real. As we can see from this chart, these feelings intensify and fade in peaks and valleys.

Intensity Phases of Bereavement

Notice the jagged peaks. The pain and grief actually intensify at three months and then gradually subside, but not steadily. They go up and down. Most people experience a rush of grief and pain at the first-year anniversary of the loss of a loved one that rivals the initial feelings. If anyone tries to tell you that you should be "over it by now" or "feeling better" at any of those peak times, you may become quite upset. That's understandable. It's also understandable that people don't appreciate the grief process unless they've been through it themselves.[4]

Time after time I've shown this chart in seminars, and people have come up and said, "Why didn't someone warn me about the three-month and one-year anniversary? It would have made it easier to handle. I thought I was going crazy!" Another problem is that most people feel that after three months of grieving a person ought to be doing all right.[5] So they pull their support away at a time when the one in grief needs it more than ever.

Death of a Parent

The first death I experienced with a family member came when I was 22. My father was killed in a traffic accident while driving home from work. He was 72. What I remember was the devastating news and shock. When my mother died in 1993 at the age of 93, it was a loss but not a shock. Her illness was gradual, and she had wanted to go home to be with the Lord for several years.

When Dad died, there was a sense of missing out on future events, especially since my wife and I discovered the week after the accident that we were going to be parents. Losing the first parent can bring a lingering pain as you constantly witness the effects of this loss on the remaining parent. And you can feel added pressure as you feel responsible in a new way for helping this parent.

When you lose a parent, you lose a person who for many years has been the most influential person in your life. For most of us, losing a parent means losing someone who loved us and cared for us in a way no one else does or ever will again. We can no longer gain their approval, praise, or permission. Feelings of attachment to a parent are unique.

When parents die, you lose your direct link to the past as well as to parts of yourself you may have forgotten. Not only that, you're much more aware of your own immortality. You feel more vulnerable because your parents aren't there to buffer life's ups and downs. When the second parent dies, it's like the last chapter of a book. For some it means they can never go home again, psychologically or physically. When you have to close up your parents' home and sort through what is left, you experience an abundance of secondary losses.

As you grow older, you often become attached to your parent in a new way. It becomes more of an adult-to-adult or friend-to-friend relationship. I've seen this in the closeness of my wife and her mother. The roles have reversed from the parent caring for the child to the child caring for the parent. And when Joyce's mother died, even though she was in her 90s and wanted the Lord to take her, it was painful for Joyce.

Responses to the death of a parent vary from person to person, depending on the quality of the relationship. If you've had a good relationship with a parent, you wish it could continue. You feel let down now that your parent has been taken away. For others, the loss is also the loss of opportunity to make up for difficulties in the past. You may feel cheated that you lost out on doing more for your parent(s).

For some there may be a sense of relief. The fear that you would someday lose your parents was a reality, and now you plan to go on with your life.

Perhaps the person to whom you were closest wasn't a birth parent. It may have been an aunt or uncle or even a surrogate parent. It's important that you face what you are feeling with this loss, experience the fullness of the grief and all the secondary losses, and then move forward in your life without the person.

Not everyone has a good relationship with his or her parents. This can complicate the grief response. In some cases I've seen a person express relief over the death of a parent. At last he or she feels a freedom from conflict and pain. For many it's a new chance at life, an opportunity not to have to try to please someone they could never please. You may feel relief from the demands you've struggled with for years. Or you may feel relief because your parent died of a lingering terminal illness that made it difficult to take care of them and drained your finances.

As you grieve the loss of a parent, keep in mind that other family members will grieve differently because of the quality of their relationship with the parent. Your siblings, spouse, and children had a different relationship than you did.

When your parents are gone, who takes their place or continues their role? Perhaps they were the peacekeepers for all the children and grandchildren. Who does that now? Perhaps they orchestrated the family get-togethers. Who takes on that role now? Decisions concerning home and property must be made and your family heirlooms divided up. The passing of parents will definitely affect your relationship with your siblings.[6] Consideration of some of these changes in advance makes it easier for the surviving member.

Death of a Sibling

One of the least talked about losses in adulthood is the death of a sibling. And if you come from a large family, you could experience more sibling deaths than other losses. There seems to be an unspoken expectation that a brother or sister's death will have very little impact upon a person. It's true that there are many variables to affect your response to a sibling's death. But let's assume you were raised with this sibling and experienced normal sibling involvement.

Losing a sibling means losing someone who was a part of your significant memories, both pleasant and unpleasant. Your sibling has been in your life as long or almost as long as your parents. His or her death can make you feel older. Someone who knew you in a unique way is gone. And if he or she was the last family member left except for you, you may begin to think about when and how you will die.

You could feel a sense of responsibility for your sibling's spouse and children. Previous trips to see them were probably based more upon seeing your brother or sister. Now that your sibling is gone, you may wonder what your role is. You may worry about losing contact to some degree. If your sibling was the favorite child or the most recognized, you may wonder whether you will assume that role and whether you will receive the same response when you die.

Death of a Child

The death of a child is unlike any other loss. It's a horrendous shock, no matter how it happens.

Years ago, when infectious diseases ran wild, childhood death was common. Today that has changed, and most deaths occur naturally and expectedly among the elderly. Our society is prepared for death with this group, and we handle it relatively well. But the pain of grieving over a child is intense, complicated, and seems to linger forever.

Many couples have grieved over the inability to have children. So many hopes and dreams have been crushed by the inability to conceive, yet too often there is little or no social recognition for this loss, and the couple has to endure the insensitive comments of others.

The death of a child through miscarriage is not recognized much in our society. Yet up to 25 percent of all pregnancies end in miscarriage. In many cases there may not have been any external signs of the pregnancy. Few people may have known about it. For those other than the parents, the child wasn't yet real.

It doesn't matter how long a mother carries her child. The intensity of the parents' grief response will be determined by their hopes, their expectations, and the meaning this child had for them. In most cases it takes six to nine months for the woman to recover emotionally from a miscarriage. Even though the child wasn't born yet, emotional bonding with the child occured.

One of the most difficult and disturbing issues to handle is the wrongness of a child's death. It just shouldn't happen. It doesn't make sense. It's death out of turn. The parents often feel, "Why should I survive when our child who should have survived us, didn't?" Death violates the cycle that children grow up and replace the old.

When you lose a child, you also lose what your child represented to you. You feel victimized in so many ways. You feel as though you've lost part of yourself. Especially painful is the loss of the child's features and characteristics that bore the most resemblance to you or your spouse.

You will miss the physical interaction—the sight, sound, smell, and touch of your child. If you were still in the hands-on caregiving stage with your child, this absence will be terribly painful.

Because of all these losses, your grief over the death of a child will be more intense and last longer than grief over the loss of any other person significant to you. The death of a child has been called the ultimate bereavement, and so it is.

As a bereaved parent, you'll have to "grow up with the loss." Parents tend to mark their lives by the events involving the accomplishments of their children. The dates when those events would have occurred will still come around, even though your child won't be there to experience them. The sixth birthday; the first teen birthday; the times when your child would have received a driver's license, graduated, married, and had children—all will bring a resurgence of your grief when you least expect it.

Our son Matthew died at the age of 22. He was a profoundly mentally retarded child and at his death was about 18 months old mentally. He lived in our home until he was 11 and then lived at Salem Christian Home in Ontario, California. At the age of 21 he developed a condition known as reflux esophagitis, a burning of the lining of the esophagus. He was given medication, but when that didn't work, Matthew went into the hospital for corrective surgery. Following the surgery, complications and infection set in. After a week had passed, additional surgery was performed.

My wife Joyce tells what happened next in her own words:

> As I visited each day, our time together was special. I patted Matthew's hand and talked to him in simple loving words. He didn't reach out and respond, but his eyes followed me as I moved about the room. It was touching to see him content and peaceful, even during his times of discomfort.
>
> I was aware of God's presence through the days at the hospital. I was reassured that He was in control, and I had a sense of being uplifted by the prayers of family and friends. I was even able to reach out to a family dealing with their son's tragic motorcycle

accident, which had caused massive trauma to his head.

After a week, additional surgery was performed. Following the operation, Matthew stayed in the intensive care unit. He was heavily sedated and unconscious. There were eight tubes in him, and he was constantly on a ventilator. He developed adult respiratory disorder syndrome. We were hopeful when the fever dropped and his blood pressure stabilized, but in several days we could see that he was not responding. The doctors felt he was in the Lord's hands. We prayed at his bedside for the Lord's will to be done.

We had stayed at our home the night of March 14 instead of at a motel near the Loma Linda Hospital. I woke up at 4:00 A.M. with the feeling that Matthew was worse. I called the hospital, and the staff confirmed my fears. They had gone to full power on the ventilator. Around 7:00 that morning as we were getting ready for the day, we received a phone call. It was one of the medical staff, and he said, "We would like you to come to the hospital as soon as possible." His request didn't need amplification.

Fortunately, we were able to speed though the traffic those 60 miles to the hospital. Both of us were aware that it could be Matthew's final hour. We had not seen any response from him for days.

Norm and I walked into the room, and the doctors told us that Matthew's lungs and heart were failing and would probably stop in about an hour. My initial response, which might surprise you if you've never had a loved one suffer and die, was profound joy. I was truly happy for him. I said, "Oh, he'll be in the presence of the Lord this day!" I knew he would be finished with the struggles of this world, totally healed, and finally out of pain.

We both felt that way. But we also felt helpless since there was nothing anyone could do to make Matthew well again. As much as we knew he was going to a far better place, we also knew we were facing the greatest loss of our lives.

We said good-bye to Matthew, and I prayed at his bedside, thanking the Lord for our precious child and for His provision of eternal life. As we stood there, we saw Matthew's pulse rate decline ten beats. We felt as though we were giving him back to God and saying, "He's Yours. Have Your perfect will with him." We believed God had something better for him.

Matthew's decreasing vital signs confirmed the reality that he was going to die soon. The doctors said we could stay there or wait in a family room, and we chose the latter. Within an hour, the doctors came to tell us Matthew had died. We cried and talked with them. God was truly loving and merciful when He took Matthew home that day, and we bowed to His perfect will. Perhaps others won't understand our mixture of feelings, but that's all right. We felt at peace.

Losing Matthew was a tremendous blow in and of itself. But like any major loss, it also caused a number of additional or secondary losses. The routine we had followed for years was gone forever. We would no longer look through catalogs to select his special sleepwear. We wouldn't have the special weekends in which he would come home and stay overnight, nor would we be able to stop by Salem to take him out to eat. Instead, we would drive past where he used to live and keep traveling along the freeway.

We faced future losses as well. Matthew would no longer be at home on Thanksgiving and Christmas, nor would we take him to Knott's Berry Farm for his birthday. Those losses we could anticipate, but each week brought others we didn't expect. (If he had been living at home, there would have been daily losses.) We couldn't call Salem anymore to see how he was doing, a topic of our conversation was gone, and certain phrases or expressions we would say to him would no longer be expressed.[7]

Even now, several years after the death of our son, Joyce and I still experience a sense of dullness or feeling down on what would have been Matthew's birthday. And when March 15 rolls around each year, we're especially sensitive, because that's the day he died.

No matter how you lose a child, questions arise: "How do I recover? What steps can I take to survive *this?*"

What can any parent do with such a loss? There is no easy way to recover. Losing a child is truly the ultimate bereavement. There are no shortcuts. You have to face your loss and let your emotions flow. God's gift of tears is more needed now than any other time. (See *Recovering from the Losses of Life* for additional help.)

Death of a Mate

Every person who marries and remains married will end up being a widow or widower (unless both die simultaneously).

No matter how the death of a mate occurs, your life is disrupted—big time. Whether the loss is a sudden accident or a prolonged illness, recovery is never easy. There is a lasting pain when you agonize over a three-year fatal disease, and there is also severe pain and shock when the officer at the door notifies you of the fatal automobile accident.

The authors of *Getting to the Other Side of Grief: Overcoming the Loss of a Spouse* said, "When a spouse dies, we really have little choice about grief. Some pretend not to grieve, but for the most part, grief rolls over the survivor like a torrent during the days and weeks following the death."[8]

One widow said, "When my husband died, it was as if a great tree had fallen in the forest and left a lonesome place against the sky." Suddenly you experience a huge hole that wasn't there before. There is a hole in your life; you no longer feel whole. A piece of you is missing. A common reaction to the death of your spouse is to feel that part of you died. And it is true that part of you did die—the part that was defined by your relationship with your spouse."[9]

Grief can begin the healing process that allows one to move forward in life without the person they loved.

Loss Through Divorce

There are other types of losses you may encounter in your life or in the lives of other family members. Your own marriage may remain intact throughout your lifetime, but that may not be the case for others in your family. Divorce is always a shock, but especially when it happens to your own children or even to your parents. Divorce turns your life, your dreams, and your ideals upside down.

I spoke with parents who had experienced the divorce of all three of their adult children. In one case, their daughter and her three children came to live with them for a year. Their adult son needed financial help, and his ex-wife moved two thousand miles away with their children. The parents' retirement and travel plans went out the window as they became involved in helping their children pull their lives back together.

When your parents divorce, it can be devastating. Much is said and written about the impact of divorce on children and adolescents. But what happens when you are in your 20s or 30s and you discover that your parents are divorcing? As one married daughter said:

> When they told me they were divorcing after 39 years of marriage, I felt like I'd been run over by a truck. Why them? Why now? I had this image of a huge building collapsing and sending its debris in every direction. For the next few weeks I walked around in a fog. My parents! I didn't know what to do or say. We'd never be together again for the holidays. Why did they do this? Didn't they know they were disrupting all of their kids' lives?

Terminal or Chronic Illness

Serious illness isn't just a crisis for the one who is ill; it also affects everyone around the ill person. Chronic illness has been likened to an octopus that reaches out and grasps everyone within reach of its tentacles and holds them for as long as the effects of the illness continue. It's also unpredictable, like a terrorist who demands everything from you that you value most—your energy, money, time, stability, peace of mind, and dreams for the future.

Many illnesses are unpredictable and constantly changing. This keeps caregivers in an upset state as well. And all this time the lives of other family members are disrupted as they attempt to carry on a somewhat normal life while caring for the sick person.

Recently I received a letter from a friend of mine. For years he was active in ministry, first as a pastor and then as the director of a national ministry. For the past several years most of his time has been divided between ministering to others and caring for his wife as she struggles with cancer. She has gone from surgery to surgery, from remission to remission.

The current letter told of her breaking both legs, having a fistula, or break, in the bowel, and finally a colostomy. He talked about the details of the daily care and the support group of faithful friends and family. He described his own ups and downs as well as concerns over his wife's eventual death. He shared his feelings of exhaustion, loss, loneliness, uselessness, and guilt. He never expected this to be a part of his life. None of us do. He survived because of his faith, his ministry to others, and a strong support network of family and friends.

Health issues can become a permanent way of life for an estimated 14 percent of the population. This number increases to 25 percent of those between ages of 46 and 65, and 45 percent of those older than 65.

When an illness is chronic, such as coma, dementia, or Alzheimer's, the loss has a sense of ambiguity. You know your loved one is going to die, but you don't know when. Some families have been known to physically shut out family members long before they die. They do this for self-protection and survival because they can't tolerate death or a lingering illness. The greater the sense of not knowing the outcome, the greater the sense of helplessness a person feels.

When a serious illness strikes, identities and family roles need to change. When family members are able to accept the reality of what is occurring and make these changes, they are able to function more effectively.

A diagnosis that strikes fear into anyone who hears it is "You have Alzheimer's." Estimates indicate there are close to three million Alzheimer's victims at the present time. Unless we find a way to prevent its onset, this number will increase to close to ten million in the next 35 years.

Alzheimer's has been called the disease of the century, not just for what it does to the victim but for the devastation it causes the victim's family and friends. Some families become powerless as they try to care for the victim. If the victim is elderly, the caregiving spouse can become an "invisible patient," succumbing prematurely to a variety of diseases often brought on by around-the-clock care. The family members experience one loss after another as they watch the progression of this disease.[10]

Ken Gire describes his visit to the small town where he spent his boyhood. He meandered around town and then went to visit his aunt, his last remaining relative there. His description of the visit captures what it is like to live with Alzheimer's.

> Now Alzheimer's.
>
> That was the worst, I think. Forgetting not simply where you put your glasses or car keys, but forgetting where you've been and where you are, forgetting who you are and

once were, whom you loved and who loved you.

Her husband and daughter wheeled her into the other room and lifted her into bed. When they returned, we talked about her condition and what doctors were doing for her or not doing, what medication she was taking and how she was reacting to it, what kind of diet she was on, things like that. She couldn't do anything for herself. Couldn't dress herself, feed herself, bathe herself. She was like a baby, only a baby that weighed something like 90 pounds, which made dressing her and bathing her and putting her to bed an exhausting ordeal. Her babbling was like a baby's, too, except at times her tone was insistent, even angry. She was declining fast and would have to be put in a nursing home, they told me.

When time came for me to leave, I went into the bedroom to say my last good-bye to an aunt who all of her life had loved me but who now no longer even knew me.

I touched her hand and stroked the soft, slack skin on her arm. "I have to leave now," I told her, trying to get her attention over the babbling. And as I reached down to hug her, the babbling stopped. "I love you," I said, as I kissed her forehead. Her frail, slack arm reached up to me, trembling with weakness, and she tried the best she could to hug me and said, "I love you too."

She remembered who I was. Maybe only for a moment, but she remembered.

> As I got into my car, tears pooled in my eyes. So this is how it all ends. This is how we slip out of this world, with all the limitations of a baby but with none of its loveliness. Every day losing a little bit of our motor skills and a little bit of our minds. Every day losing more of our balance and losing more control of our bowels. Every day losing a little something else until at last there's nothing to lose except life itself.[11]

As long as a person lives like Ken's aunt, there is suffering. This disease is just one of many that some will have to face. Loss and family membership go hand in hand. This is life. It's better to be aware of the possibility of such losses and prepare for the unexpected, especially the uninvited.

Just remember that along with the pain of loss there can be growth. We will be different. Pain offers an opportunity to "grow into the likeness of Christ." It can produce maturity in our lives...if we let it.

> Moreover [let us also be full of joy now!] Let us exult and triumph in our troubles and rejoice in our sufferings, knowing that pressure and affliction and hardship produce patient and unswerving endurance. And endurance (fortitude) develops maturity of character, (approved faith and tried integrity). And character [of this sort] produces [the habit of] joyful and confident hope of eternal salvation.
>
> ROMANS 5:3-4 AMP

6

"Mommy, It Hurts!"

Children—The Forgotten Grievers

When does loss begin for any human being? It begins when we're children—during those years when we're most vulnerable.

Do you remember the losses of your childhood? That's when you first became acquainted with loss, even though you may not always have identified what you experienced as loss. Because many children don't identify their losses as such, they fail to grieve over their experiences. Some childhood losses are obvious; others are less so. Some are blatant, while others are subtle. Some experiences are not just a loss—they're a crisis or even a trauma.

Life is a continual blending of loss and gain. Some losses are necessary for normal growth. For instance, a child discovers a tooth that is starting to wiggle loose. Soon it either falls out or is pulled. But the child learns that this loss is necessary to make room for the permanent tooth. The child loses a baby tooth but gains a permanent tooth (and sometimes a little money under the pillow). But then major losses occur—far more serious than the loss of a tooth—some of which may be traumatic to the child.

The following are the most common childhood losses, in the sequence most likely to occur in a child's life: death of a pet; death of a grandparent; a major move; divorce of a child's parents; death of a parent(s); death of a playmate, friend, or relative; debilitating injury to the child or to someone important in the child's life. Were any of these part of your childhood experience?[1]

The Impact of Childhood Loss

The way we learn to handle losses in childhood impacts our lives as adults. The losses of adult life may actually be compounded by some of the unresolved losses of our childhood. These are brought into adult life like unwelcome baggage. And in time, this baggage could turn an adult loss into a crisis. Losses vary in their complexity and intensity. For instance, some children are never allowed or encouraged to grieve over the loss of their favorite pet. Instead, they're told, "Don't cry. It's just a cat," or "We'll get you a new goldfish tomorrow."

A family move can be a major loss for a child. A friend saying, "I don't want to play with you anymore" is a loss. Not making the Little League team, or simply not getting to play in the big game can devastate a child. Not having a favorite dress available for a special day can be devastating for an adolescent girl. Not getting the part in a school play can spoil an entire week for some kids. Caring adults need to see losses through the eyes of the child—not through their more hardened adult eyes.

Sometimes the loss results from an unexplained withdrawal of involvement on the part of the parents. When Ken was a child, both of his parents were actively involved in all of his soccer, Little League, and school activities. But when he turned 11, they not only stopped attending his activities, but they didn't even ask him about them. No explanation was given; he couldn't understand it and ached inside for some response on their part. But it never came. This disappointment led to a fear that *everyone will end up doing this to me,* and consequently, a sense of caution and suspicion began to develop within Ken which later affected his relationships as an adult.

More and more people enter adulthood with a sense of loss because they were children of divorce. *Newsweek* magazine estimated that 45 percent of all children will live with only one parent at some time before they turn 18. The results of studies on children of divorce indicate that the effects of divorce on a child are more serious and long-lasting than many parents are willing to admit. And more school-age children will lose a parent to divorce than to death. Self-blame for the loss (and the resulting feelings of guilt) are higher in divorced children than they are in bereaved children.[2]

These children of divorce also tend to leave school sooner than children from stable families. In New York City, which has a very high adolescent suicide rate, two out of every three teenage suicides occur among teenagers whose parents are divorced. Many others carry a pattern of insecurity, depression, anxiety, and anger into their adult years because of the loss they experienced. Divorce results in a multitude of losses for the affected child. These include not only the disruption of the family unit, but also the possible permanent loss of one of the parents, the home, neighborhood, school, friends, standard of living, family outings, family holidays, self-esteem...and the list goes on.

When a parent dies, there is a sense of closure to the relationship and an opportunity to say a final good-bye. Of course, children go through an important period and sequence of mourning. But the mourning period after a divorce is open-ended. It comes and goes depending upon the involvement of the non-custodial parent. If the parent does not stay involved, the children wonder if Mom or Dad will ever come back. And if not, then *why not?* The children will question what they have done to cause this situation. They will question if the loss is permanent or temporary. The occasional birthday card, the weekly phone call, and the all-too-infrequent visits and vacations tend to keep the fantasy alive that the parent might return home.

The Loss of Abuse

In recent years, we've been hearing more and more about childhood physical and sexual abuse. This is not just a loss that will contaminate a child's adulthood—it's a trauma. Abuse is demeaning, it takes away the innocence of children, and it distorts their perception of adults. Victims of abuse often learn to suffer silently, having lost the love of a parent, their dreams, and their innocence. In essence, they've lost their childhood.

Another damaging childhood loss is abandonment. While it's true that some children are physically abandoned, many more children are *emotionally* abandoned. Often kids don't know why they feel so alone and rejected. Their parents may be physically present and their bodily needs are met— but their emotional needs are neglected. They lack nurturing, hugging, and the emotional intimacy necessary for healthy emotional development. The verbal affirmations they so desperately need are shrouded in silence. Soon they begin to think that something is wrong with them, and they carry this misperception into their adulthood. Teenagers are particularly vulnerable to parental silence because they often seem to want to be left alone, causing parents to withdraw. But the truth is, teens need constant reassurance of their parents' love and attention.

Time after time I have seen the ungrieved losses of childhood impair an adult's ability to respond normally to life and relationships. Perhaps your own adult relationships have been affected by the losses of your childhood.

Two Stages of Crisis Resolution

What if the loss is a crisis or a trauma for a child?

Children cope with crisis events in a different way from adults. They are more limited in their coping skills.

For children, there are two stages of crisis resolution. The first-stage reaction involves the initial shock and then a high level of anxiety. Adults handle this anxiety better because of their previous experience with crisis. Normally children do not have a wealth of experience to draw upon. They do not know that their problem will be resolved, and they feel as though they are in the midst of a tornado. The child's mind and emotional state are not yet developed enough to solve problems as an adult would. Adults can fall back on resources and established routines—children fall back on *chaos*. In a way they lose their identity or sense of self as they are enveloped in this chaotic tornado.

The second stage is similar but less intense. The child's reaction is less crippling, and he or she is able to look at the crisis and evaluate it instead of just responding to it.

But children often lack the verbal skills and the creative fantasy available to an adult. They may find a *poor* solution and cling to it even though it is not good for them. For this reason, children need to be able to discuss and sort out their fears with a caring adult who can help them realize they have better options than they can see.

If children remain anxious and don't live up to their potential, they are stuck in the second stage and haven't yet resolved their crisis. In uncontrollable events, children feel helpless. When they experience helplessness repeatedly, they learn to despair at their inability to be in control. Children with repeated experiences of loss of control soon lose control totally. Some adults are capable of handling crisis by restricting their activities in some way, but this approach is not available to children. They must face daily challenges—for instance, they are not allowed to skip school whenever they choose as a means of coping with adversity.

One of the characteristic responses of children under crisis is regression. When children respond at their appropriate age level, they know how to use their skills and capabilities properly to relate to others and confront daily tasks. But in a crisis, they may become upset and lose their capability to coordinate all their abilities to meet the needs of the situation. They become confused, disorganized, off-balance. Those attempting to help them may need to take charge of part of their life and guide their behavior temporarily.[3]

Direct Trauma and Vicarious Trauma

Some children experience trauma directly. It happens at school, in the streets, and for many even at home. Children and teens are victims in many places like Oklahoma City, Columbine, Wedgewood in Fort Worth, and the Trade Towers in New York City. Can you imagine sitting in the Premiere High School or elementary school in Manhattan, looking out the windows to see airplanes crashing into the towers a few hundred yards away? And within minutes you're rushing out the school doors, hoping to escape far enough away from the destruction to survive. You make it to safety, but you learn that the sister of the principal of your high school, as well as others you know, died in the tower.

When the elementary school reopened its doors, the students in one of the classes came to their schoolroom and just sat and stared. They weren't able to function. The father of one of their classmates worked in the towers. They had seen him before. But they wouldn't again. If we as adults struggle with thoughts, feelings, and images after such events, what must it be like for a child?

Other children experience trauma *vicariously*. The media saturation of disasters in our country via television, newspaper, and radio has left its mark. A new term has been coined to describe the result—*Living Room Witnesses.*

We used to say that in the United States few children experience human-perpetrated disasters. The Oklahoma City bomb blast in 1995 signaled a change which was greatly amplified by the Trade Tower disaster of September 11, 2001. Since these two events, there are few children in America who haven't been exposed to catastrophes through the media. The repetitious viewing of these events, especially the planes impacting the Twin Towers and their collapse, tattooed these destructive images on the minds of the children who sat transfixed in front of their television sets. *USA Today* told of preschool children building towers out of Legos and then crashing toy planes into them again and again saying, "They're dead. All the people are dead." A mother on Long Island, New York, told me about her preschooler who built cardboard towers each day and silently crashed his planes into them. Adults share their fears and concerns over these events with us during the day; the children live with them at night.

The Messages of Trauma

Traumatic events of any kind turn the life of a child upside down. To a youngster, a trauma is a wound like an ongoing, festering splinter.

Trauma sends four messages to children:

- ❧ Your world is no longer safe.
- ❧ Your world is no longer kind.
- ❧ Your world is no longer predictable.
- ❧ Your world is no longer trustworthy.

It's difficult enough for adults to handle these negative messages, but children don't have the mental or verbal ability or the life experiences to draw on for hope. A child's mind doesn't work the same way as an adult's. It's less sophisticated and processes information about tragic events differently than adults. To a child, trauma brings silence, isolation, and a feeling of helplessness.

So what do children need in a trauma? An abundance of them need to be encouraged to be patient with themselves and their reactions. They need to be reassured repeatedly that it's all right to feel and express the feelings they have.

Children are the forgotten grievers in our country. During a crisis, adults seem to receive the lion's share of the attention, and children are often left out of the equation—as if they don't experience grief. But they not only do experience grief, their grief is unique. Children of crisis *need* to grieve.

Features of a Child's Grief

There are several unique features of a child's grief:

- It comes out in the middle of everyday life. It can't be predicted.

- They can put grief aside easier than adults can. One question may be about their grandfather's death, and the next is about their doll.

- It comes out in brief but intense episodes.

- They express their grief in actions. They're limited in their verbal expression.

- They often postpone their grief or part of it.

- Childhood grief often lasts throughout childhood, and remnants of it last into adulthood.

- Children grieve differently from adults. Instead of experiencing ongoing intense distress, many children are likely at first to deny death, then grieve intermittently for many years.

This is why it's so critical to *communicate* with a child in crisis.

Information is crucial, and its impartation to a child can solve many troubling issues:

- It tames fears. By talking with children about death and grief, you can recreate a secure place so they can learn to trust the world again.

- Information restores to children a sense of control. During crisis, they feel confused and besieged by new emotions. They need to be anchored by caring adults.

- Information gives children permission to express feelings they want to communicate. Children don't grieve on command. They need the freedom to come to adults who care for them at any time.

- Information helps children prepare for future losses. Sheltered children can't cope as well as those who understand the truth that life involves occasional losses.

If you don't talk to them, they'll talk to themselves and fill in the blanks! A child's imagination and playmates are not good resources.[4]

It's important to identify what may hinder a child from grieving the losses he or she may experience. The following factors most often contribute to this problem:

- The parents have difficulty grieving past or current losses.

- The parents are unable to handle and accept their children's expressions of pain. They don't know how to respond.

- The children are worried about how the parents are handling the loss and attempt to protect them.

- The children are overly concerned with maintaining control and feeling secure and may feel frightened or threatened by the grief.

- The parent does not caringly prod, stimulate, and encourage the children to grieve.

- The children don't have the security of a loving, caring environment.

- In the case of a loved one's death, children may question their role in making it happen. Their misplaced guilt is further enhanced if they have ambivalent feelings toward the loved one.

- The family fails to acknowledge and discuss the reality of death or loss.[5]

Regardless of the type of loss children experience, the following steps are important in the grieving process:

- Children need to *accept* the loss, *experience* the pain, and *express* their sorrow.

- Children require assistance to identify and express the wide range of feelings they're experiencing.

- Children need to know why you are sad, why others are sad, and why they are sad. This lets your children know that it's *okay* to be sad. Tell them, "This is how we feel when someone dies."

- Children must be told that it is the death that has made you sad. Without an explanation they may think your sadness is caused by something they did or didn't do. Start by saying, "This is a very, very sad time..."; "A very, very sad thing has happened..."; "Mommy and Daddy are sad because..."

- In the case of death, children need encouragement to remember and review their relationship with the loved one.

- Children need help in learning to relinquish and say good-bye to what they have lost.

- Children also respond differently to loss depending on their age and level of emotional maturity.

The Age Factor

Grieving occurs even in very young infants. Young children between four months and two years of age express distress when responding to a loss. At this stage, separation from Mom is a significant loss. If the separation is sudden, the child will express shock and protest. Prolonged separation creates despair and sadness. The child loses interest in objects and activities that are usually pleasurable. Unless a caring individual steps into the vacated role, the infant will become detached from everyone.

Ages Two to Five

Children between two and five years old may show their grief in a number of ways. Because they don't understand the significance of the loss, they may ask seemingly useless questions again and again. They may ask questions such as, "Hasn't he been dead long enough?" Learning concepts takes time for children, and death is a concept that hasn't been formed yet in the minds of very young children. They may appear bewildered and tend to regress in their behavior, becoming demanding and clinging. If what was lost is not returned, expressions of anger increase. An adult may need to assist children to acknowledge and express feelings of loss. Many people make the mistake of removing children from familiar surroundings following a family death or trauma. This further undermines their sense of security and raises their anxiety.

In the case of death, children at this age are obsessed with thoughts of the lost loved one and are overwhelmed by an intense sadness. They tend to idealize this person, continually reviewing and remembering their lost relationship.

Ages Three to Six

Children between the ages of three and six years old engage in what is known as magical thinking. They believe that their own thoughts can influence people and events. For instance, a child who is upset about a parent taking a trip may wish the car would have a flat tire so the parent wouldn't leave. Then, when the parent is killed in a car crash caused by a blowout, the child feels responsible—in his mind, his wish killed the parent.

During this age, children's fears increase. They become aware of threatening events in the world around them. They're curious about bodily functions. When they experience the death of a loved one, children may ask questions such as: "Can he still eat?" "Can he go potty?" "Does he cry?" "Will he get out of the box and hug me again?" "Will he be a ghost?"

At this age, children don't understand the permanency of death. To them, death is reversible. E.T. came back from the dead. So did Jesus and Lazarus. And so does the Coyote on the *Roadrunner* cartoons. If you wish hard enough, a person will come back to life. When a pet dies, young children may act as if it is still alive by calling it, asking to feed it, or looking under a bed for it. These kids see people and animals as cartoon characters—able to survive anything. To them, death is merely a deep and temporary sleep. Parents often reinforce this misconception by telling them that the dead person is *resting* or *just didn't wake up*. Even some of the terminology used by funeral homes reinforces the denial of the permanency of death—*the slumber room,* for example.[6]

Young children are focused on themselves. They often fail to take into account the viewpoints and beliefs of others. They engage in their own private language, often talking past each other. They're unable to distinguish between themselves as the speaker and someone else as the listener. They assume their words carry more meaning than they actually do, and they have little concern whether the listener understands or not. At this age, children are very literal and can easily be confused by statements such as "Don't pull my leg," "That's a bunch of baloney," "Keep your shirt on," "Don't give up the ship," or "Hang in there." This begins to change at around seven years of age.

Young children often make their own unique connections. They tend to group objects, events, and people together in a way that makes sense to them but not to anyone else. For example, Tom's grandfather had a stroke while at a baseball game with him. Now, Tom becomes anxious whenever he visits the neighborhood playground because it's next to a baseball field. His parents, though, don't understand what's wrong with him.

Children in this age-group often focus their attention on one detail of an experience and ignore everything else. They have difficulty seeing the whole picture clearly. Thus they don't comprehend the significance of loss.

If Grandpa dies, they may ask or think,

    Does this mean someone else is going to die?

    Grandpa died from a headache. Mommy says she has a headache too...

   🕿 *Old people die. Daddy is very old—Daddy may die too...*

Be prepared for indirect questions, aimed at finding out if someone else might die:

"How old are you? How old is Daddy?"

You must explain the difference between:

   🕿 *very, very sick and just "sick"*

   🕿 *very, very old and over 20*

   🕿 *very old and very sick and very old and not sick*[7]

As children get older they develop the ability to understand loss and even death. But even then, they're vulnerable because although they can grasp the significance of their losses, they still have limited skills to cope with them.

If there is a death, they often look on it as a "Taker," something that comes and gets you. The question, "Who killed him?" is common. They may accept death as a reality, but not accept the fact that everyone is going to die. One of the worst prayers that has been taught to children over the years (including me) was

Now I lay me down to sleep,
I pray the Lord my soul to keep;
If I should die before I wake,
I pray the Lord my soul to take.

What damage did this do to many young children?

When faced with loss, children may use denial as a coping mechanism. It's easier to act as if nothing has happened. Children may also hide their feelings at this age because they don't want to look like a baby. Afraid of becoming out of control, children may vent their feelings only when alone. To others, they may appear insensitive, uncaring, and unaffected by the loss, leaving the parent unaware of the extent of their grief. At this age, children need to be encouraged again and again to express their feelings. Allowing your children to see you grieve and talking about your own feelings can help them work though their grief.

In order to cope with their loss, kids live in a fantasy world of their own making. Morbid thoughts are common. In an effort to maintain the pre-existing relationship with whatever or whomever they lost, these children use fantasy as an escape. They may tend to idealize the qualities of the loved one, and other members of the family don't fare as well when compared to their idealized fantasies.

Ages Five to Eight

Five through eight year olds can experience a variety of feelings during loss ranging from misplaced guilt to embarrassment about being in some way different from their peers. They often feel pressure to be strong and self-reliant because of their fear for themselves and their concern for other family members. They may become more helpful than usual in order to shut out the pain of their loss and to feel more in control.

Ages Nine to Twelve

Children between the ages of nine and twelve years old experience dramatic changes in their thinking. They develop conceptual thinking and problem-solving skills. They relate more to real-life people and events than to a fantasy or make-believe world. They begin to understand the meaning and ramifications of loss. If the loss is a death, they are now able to reflect on the consequences of death, and that becomes evident in their questions. They may ask, "What will happen to Frieda now?" "Who will take care of her grandfather?" "Will Bill have to move now?" Even though their thinking is more developed, they jump to conclusions. They don't always understand what they hear, especially if it's communicated to them in adult terminology. Adults need to communicate clearly to these children using simple statements, repeating and rephrasing important points of the message.[8]

Children at this age are becoming more independent, but they are still fragile. In fact, they may exhibit some of the same responses as their younger counterparts. They struggle with feelings of helplessness and childishness but don't want others to know, so they often put up a façade of coping with their losses even though they recognize the finality and irreversibility of losing someone or something they love. Thus, their grief remains unresolved.

One of the main reasons children at this age have difficulty grieving—or often become stuck in their grief—is because their parents aren't always honest with them about losses. They attempt to shield their children from pain and don't encourage them to grieve or teach them *how* to grieve. If parents shield their children from a loss, especially a family loss, their emotional development will be stunted. They must be included when the family grieves.

It's also important to understand the *way* children grieve. Children don't have an adult's capacity to tolerate intense pain for a long period of time. They are more likely to grieve intermittently, mourning the loss for a while, playing a short time, then returning to the grief. If children experience the loss of a parent at this age, they may mirror a symbolic behavior associated with that parent. Or some children may try to act grown-up to mask their feelings of pain and helplessness. These children are easy to spot—they become "little adults" who try to care for everyone else, or they act bossy and controlling. Given the right setting, these children's fears become phobias, and their physical concerns obsessive.

Most children at this age have limited opportunities to express their grief. Unfortunately, most of us have not been instructed in grief, so we tend to avoid those who are struggling with loss, or we end up making a lot of useless, inappropriate remarks. But our kids depend upon caring adults to help them work through their losses. They lack the developmental experiences that assure them that the pain of a loss will ease in time and go away. As parents, we need to encourage them to express their feelings and give them the confidence that they will survive the loss.

Given the right support and guidance, most children will be able to handle and recover from both the minor and the significant losses in their lives. In fact, the process can provide valuable learning experiences as they mature to adulthood.

"What Can a Grown-up Do to Help?"

Guidelines to Help Children Grieve

The death of a loved one is an extremely difficult loss for anyone to handle. But for children, it's even more difficult because they lack the resources to deal with such a serious loss. Let's consider the reactions of children to a loss such as death.

Fear

Children who experience the death of a loved one can experience a number of fears, including

- Fear of losing the other parent, siblings, or grandparents—they tend to see the remaining people as candidates for death.

- Fear of their own death—this is especially true if the child was younger than a sibling who died, and this child is approaching the age at which the sibling died.

🐾 Fear of going to sleep because they equate sleep with death—even the prayer, "If I should die before I wake…" reinforces this misconception. Dreams and nightmares intensify the fear.

🐾 Fear of separation because of the perceived insecurity of the home and family—they no longer feel safe and protected. And they're hesitant to talk about their feelings because it may upset the other family members. One young girl told me, "When Daddy died, I wanted to talk to my mother about it. But I was afraid to because it made her cry, and I didn't want the others yelling at me 'cause I did that."

Guilt

Another feeling associated with grief is guilt. It's difficult to identify all of the sources of guilt, but there seem to be three main reasons children experience guilt when a loved one dies:

1. *They died because I did something wrong. I misbehaved!*
   Children have a knack for remembering things they've done that they think were wrong. They may have made a mistake, broken something, or forgotten to say or do something. Just like adults, children can end up with an incredible list of *if onlys* or regrets.

2. *I wanted them dead. I thought it and it happened.*
   It's important to remember that young children believe they can actually make things happen by thinking them. It's easy for kids to think their anger or aggression killed the loved one. Because they

take on this responsibility, they live in fear of being found out and punished.

3. *I didn't love them enough.*
It's common for children to believe that if you love someone enough, it will keep them from dying. They long for a second chance to make things right.

Anger

Another common grief response is anger. During a loss there are many potential triggers for a child's anger. They often feel abandoned and left to face life on their own. They're angry because their future has been dramatically changed—they won't be with that special person anymore. They feel victimized by events that are out of their control. Children may be angry at their parents

- for not telling them that the person who died was so sick.

- for spending so much time with the sick person. They feel neglected and isolated.

- just because they need someone to be angry with[1]

Kids may express this anger in different ways. It may be targeted like a well-aimed bullet or sprayed in all directions like shotgun pellets. It may be directed at family members, friends, teachers, pets, or even at God. It may be expressed in tantrums, fights, silent hostility, or verbal blasts. As difficult as it may be to experience these demonstrative expressions of anger, they are healthy signs. The alternative response—bottling up their anger—can result in many physical and emotional problems.

Confusion

Worth mentioning here is the confusion that can accompany the loss of a loved one. Just imagine that you are a six-year-old child who has been raised in a Christian home and your mother dies. You will probably wonder, *Where is God? Why didn't He keep my mother alive? Why didn't He make her well? My uncle told me Mom went to be with God. Why'd He do that?* Not only are children confused about God, but they are dealing with a mixture of feelings about the person who died.

They're also trying to sort through the mixed messages and advice they receive from grown-ups, whose expectations often create additional confusion. One adult may be implying, *Oh, you poor little child. You must feel so sad and alone.* At the same time, someone else may be giving the message, *Now you're the man in the family. You'll have to be strong.* The child can be confused by these conflicting messages that say to be strong, sad, in control, able to help others, willing to let others help, and so on.

The child's memories of the deceased can also cause confusion. The survivors are talking about this person in a way that conflicts with the child's memories. They are praising and lauding her perfect qualities in a way the child cannot understand. The child may wonder, *Was Mom really as perfect as they say? I didn't know that. Sometimes I didn't even like her, and I thought she was bad when she yelled and went on and on. Maybe I was wrong. I hope no one finds out what I think.* You can see how this would create confusion as well as guilt for the child.

The mood fluctuations of others can also generate confusion. Individuals around the child may be cheerful one moment and moody and quiet the next. While this is a normal response, the child is seeking stability and assurance from these people, and their changing moods cause her to question her own responses. She may ask herself, *Is it me? Did I do something wrong? Do they want me around or not?*[2]

Points to Remember: When a Parent Dies

- 🕸 The emotional responses and behaviors of children vary around the time of loss. They are strongly influenced by the reactions of the surviving parent as well as other adults.

- 🕸 When a parent is in a terminal condition, the least likely to know are the younger children.

- 🕸 Over time, most children learn to recapture memories of the funeral or memorial service and talk about it without sadness.

- 🕸 Children who are prepared for the funeral or memorial service are better able to handle it than those who weren't given any prior information.

- 🕸 Allowing children to participate in the planning of the funeral or memorial service has a positive effect. It helps them to feel important and useful at a time when many are feeling overwhelmed.

- 🕸 Children who are involved in planning the final services want them to reflect the life of the parent rather than to focus on the loss itself or the afterlife.

- 🕸 Children should be allowed to choose whether they will attend the wake, funeral, or burial. But these need to be informed choices, with children prepared for what they will see and experience.

- 🕸 Visiting the grave helps children remain connected with the dead parent. There's a huge vacancy in their life. This is a time when they are working through the new place the deceased parent has in their current life.[3]

Children should be told what is going to happen and what they are going to experience. Should they be brought to the funeral home and/or service? Definitely—if they are well prepared in advance. Tell them what will happen, then give them the choice of going or not. Fit the following explanation around your family's plans and special traditions.

_____ will be taken from _____, where he died, to the funeral home. At the funeral home _____ will be dressed in clothes that he liked and put into a casket. A casket is a box we use so that when _____ is buried, no dirt will get on him. Because _____'s body isn't working any more, it won't move or do any of the things it used to do. But it will look like _____ always did.

People will come and visit us and say how sorry they are that _____ died. After _____ days the casket will be closed and taken to the church, where people will say prayers for the family. Then we will go to the cemetery where _____ will be buried in a place that _____ picked out.

If you like, you can come to the funeral home and visit for a while—even go to the cemetery. You could bring something to leave with _____ if you want; that would be nice.

We have to go to the funeral home to make plans, and we'll let you know all about them when we come back. We will be gone _____ hours.

For cremation, use this additional information:

> After we leave the funeral home, _____ will be taken to a crematory, a place where his body will be turned into ashes. Then we will take those ashes and _____ (scatter them; keep them in an urn). Since _____'s body doesn't work and doesn't feel anything, being cremated doesn't hurt.

- If the dead person has changed because of illness or accident, it's important to describe some of this change. ("It's still Grandpa, but you know he was sick and lost a lot of weight, so he will look thinner...").[4]

- Children who remained connected after the loss are better able to talk about the dead parent. They can talk to family members as well as to others. And they are likely to try to please the dead parent with their behavior.

- It's important to have a relationship with the dead parent. This is part of the continuing process called "constructing."

- The constructing process involves discovering the meaning of this loss rather than just "letting go" of their parent. This discovering continues to be a part of the child's life experience.[5]

Here are some examples of how to describe to young children how and why a death occurred.

1. *Old Age*
   "When a person gets very, very, very old, his body wears out and stops working..."

2. *Terminal Illness*
"Because the disease couldn't be stopped, the person got very, very sick. His body wore out and stopped working..."

3. *Accident*
"A terrible thing happened (car crash, etc.); his body was badly hurt and couldn't be fixed. It stopped working..."

4. *Miscarriage*
"Sometimes when a baby is just starting to grow, something happens that makes it stop. We don't know what it was; it wasn't anything anyone did..."

5. *Stillborn*
"Sometimes something makes the baby die before it is born. We're not sure why, but it's nothing anybody did or didn't do..."

6. *Sudden Infant Death Syndrome (SIDS)*
"Sometimes with little babies something makes their bodies stop working. It's nothing anybody did or forgot to do. Doctors are not sure why it happens..."[6]

Steps to Help a Grieving Child

How can we help our children learn to handle the losses of life? Start early. Overprotection and denial robs our children of the opportunity to develop the coping skills they'll need throughout their lives.

1. *Give your children permission to grieve, and encourage them to talk and ask questions.*

Whether the loss is the death of a family member, a major move, or the loss of a pet, your children need permission to mourn. For certain kids, permission may not be enough. Some kids need an invitation to share their feelings, but they also need to be taught how to express sorrow. A few sensitive, well-directed questions can draw them out. If your children still cannot talk, don't force it. Just let them know that you are available and ready to listen when they want to talk. Look for other ways for them to express what they're feeling.

Once your children begin to talk about their feelings, it may seem like you've untapped a gusher. They are, in their limited capacity, attempting to make sense of what has happened and regain their security. Children whose questions are answered and who are given a forum for discussion have less need to fantasize and are much easier to help than are non-expressive children. If your children don't share their feelings, watch for indirect questions or statements of concern and try to put their feelings into words for them.[7]

2. *Be available when your children are ready to grieve.*
Being available may be the most important element in helping your children grieve. Remember, they need affection and a sense of security. Touching them and making eye contact will provide comfort and reassurance. Let your children know that it's normal to have ups and downs when grieving. Help them break the mourning into manageable pieces so they don't become overwhelmed. Using illustrations and word pictures can help them identify and talk about their feelings.

It may surprise you to find that your children will have the same range of emotions as you do. These emotions include anger, panic, numbness, sadness, and guilt. Children need their parents' help to identify their feelings and the sources of those feelings, and to express them in constructive ways. Following are some of the ways you can help them do this.

3. *How do you handle a child asking the same question over and over again or asking you "Why?" after every answer you give them?*
Remember their age. They can't grasp what an adult can, and if we respond with adult answers to a child's questions

it will be over their head. And if they're in a state of shock or crisis, their thinking ability is lessened even more.

It's important that children ask questions and receive simple, concrete answers.

4. *Give them opportunities for creative expression.*

Children who have difficulty verbalizing their feelings may find it easier to express them on paper. Drawing is an effective way for kids to gain control over their emotional pain and gradually deflate it. When the loss is a death, drawing is especially important because it allows kids to actually see what their feelings look like. That helps give them a sense of understanding and control.

Writing or journaling is also beneficial for children whose writing skills are developed. It's easier for kids to express on paper the reality of what's happened and their fantasies about it. Writing a letter to the deceased person or even to God can also be helpful. Encourage your children to read aloud and talk about what they've written. But remember to respect their privacy. The choice needs to be theirs.

5. *Create opportunities for play.*

Periodically your children need to be encouraged to take a break from their grief and to play with friends. Play is an important type of expression for children, especially for younger children whose verbal skills are limited. In the safety of play, a child can release various feelings. Play helps them regain a feeling of safety and security. It gives them a feeling of power over the effects of loss and allows them to separate themselves from what has happened.[8]

They may feel like they're betraying the deceased if they have fun or allow themselves some enjoyment. But play is a normal and beneficial part of their lives and gives them time to recuperate. It also helps them realize that life goes on.

6. *Watch your expectations.*

We need to be careful not to overprotect our children. Lecturing or making decisions for them is not helpful while they're coping with a loss. When possible, it's better if they learn to make their own choices and be allowed to grow through the experiences of their lives.

The flip side of this issue, though, is that adults often have expectations that are inappropriate for their children's age level. I've overheard parents or other relatives say, "You're going to have to take over now and be the man of the family (or be the strong one)." This is an unrealistic expectation and places too much of a burden on the child. These kinds of messages will short-circuit the child's grieving process. Be careful to give them age-appropriate responsibilities.

7. *Dismiss their myths.*

It's important to discover if your children are practicing magical thinking. Younger children are particularly vulnerable to this. For instance, your child may have argued with a friend, and three hours later, the friend was killed in a car accident. Your child may feel responsible. One young girl told her dog to drop dead, and the next morning it was dead. She thought she made it happen. Children tend to feel they cause things to happen with their thoughts. It's important to identify and correct these myths as soon as possible.

Kids will often be impatient with themselves because they feel sad longer than they think they should. They also feel that no one has ever felt the way they do, so they may be uncomfortable around their friends. They need to be taught not to expect too much of themselves or others at this time, and to be encouraged to talk with their friends—especially those who have experienced similar losses.

8. *Make honesty a policy.*

While grieving, our children look to us for hope and encouragement. When they ask us questions, we need to avoid giving them platitudes, and instead, let them know it's all right to question *why* bad things happen. We need to admit to them that we don't have all the answers, but that we'll get through the current crisis together. One mother told her six-year-old, "I know it is a sad time for you. We are all sad and wish things were different. There are many changes happening right now, but in time things will settle down. Someday the pain will go away. It may go away gradually and keep returning again and again, but as we help and love one another, it is going to go away.[9]"

When a family member or friend dies, ask yourself if this is your child's first experience with death. If it is, your child will need your help to understand the loss and sort out his or her feelings about it. Be especially sensitive to the child's reactions and anticipate the unexpected. Use words and phrases the child can easily understand. It may help to rehearse what you plan to say with someone else first.

Always be as clear and factual as possible, telling the truth about the death and what caused it. When kids ask questions, give them accurate information such as, "Your brother's heart stopped beating and that is why he died." It's better to use proper death language such as "Grandpa died," rather than, "Grandpa passed away." But be sensitive about how many details you give. If you have no answer to their questions, say so. Let them know, though, that when you do, you will share it with them.

In her book *Helping a Child Understand Death*, author Linda Volga suggests that when parents are questioned about death, they tell their children something like:

> We miss Grandpa, but we can be glad Grandpa doesn't hurt or feel sad anymore. His body is in the ground. Grandpa is with God and we believe God will love him and care for him in a way more beautiful and wonderful than we can imagine. When people say Grandpa is in heaven, this is what they mean.[10]

Dan Schaefer and Christine Lyons, authors of *How Do We Tell the Children?* offers an example of this type of questioning and how to respond.

- "Will Grandpa ever move again?" (No, his body has stopped working.)

- "Why can't they fix him?" (Once the body stops working, it can't start again.)

- "Why is he cold?" (The body only stays warm when it's working.)

- "Why isn't he moving?" (He can't move because his body isn't working anymore.)

- "When will he come back?" (He won't. People who die don't come back.)

- "Is he sleeping?" (No. When we sleep, our body is still working, just resting.)

- "Can he hear me?" (No. He could only hear you if his body was working.)

- "Can he eat after he is buried?" (No, a person eats only when his body is working.)[11]

9. *Allow your children to respond in their own way.*

Don't expect your kids to respond as you do. Initially, they may not seem upset or sad. Young children may even have difficulty remembering the deceased. You may need to help them remember their relationship with the deceased before they can resolve their grief. Photos and videos may be helpful. Reminiscing about times spent together and reviewing certain qualities of the person may also be helpful.

Children often regress because they don't know how to grieve.[12] The important thing is to allow children to progress at their own rates. Just be available, or have someone else available, to observe their reactions. If they begin to express strong feelings, don't block them. Allow them to cry or express anger or even bitterness. In time, they will probably begin to ask questions. Answer them simply and honestly, even though you may struggle with them yourself.

10. *Watch your children for signs of fear.*

Your children need reassurance that their family still exists, and that they are important parts of it. Children will tend to ask the same questions over and over again. Their questioning may become intense as they attempt to assimilate what has happened and how it will affect their lives. You may need an abundance of patience to answer them again and again in a loving way.[13]

Children may become especially aware of their vulnerability to losing other important people or things as they evaluate how this loss will affect their lives. Anything of importance to them could become the object of fear. It could be their home, school, friends, church, pets, a daily routine, an activity, or another loved one. They will require constant and consistent reassurance. And it's important to tell kids that if there are any planned changes in the future, these changes will be discussed with them in advance.

11. *Encourage children to continue normal family routines.*

Routines provide security and let kids know there are certain constants in their lives—things they can rely on to stay the same.

One of the most practical things parents can do is to encourage their children to take good care of themselves—to get plenty of rest and exercise and to eat a balanced diet.

Loss is a natural and inevitable part of life. Learning to deal with the feelings associated with loss and growing through the experience are key elements in your children's emotional development. Parents who guide their kids through the troubled waters of the grieving process will equip them to handle the losses of their adult lives.

"Will My Life Ever Be the Same?"

When Time Doesn't Heal All Wounds

Alice Hawthorne was a sales representative for a cable company, and she owned her own business as well. She had served in the Air Force, acted as a campaign manager for many of the candidates in the Georgia House of Representatives, and was highly thought of in her neighborhood and city. But on July 27, 1996 Alice made a simple, innocent decision that cost her her life.

It was the ninth day of the 1996 Summer Olympics and there was a free concert in Centennial Olympic Park that evening. Alice and her 14-year-old daughter were two of the thousands of visitors who decided to gather for the fun and festivity.

Little did Alice or anyone else suspect that within a few days her picture would be spread across the nation in newspapers and magazines. One minute her life was full; the next minute her life was *gone*. Alice Hawthorne was the only person killed by a bomb that exploded in Centennial Park in downtown Atlanta. More than a hundred others were wounded by the blast, including Alice's daughter who must now live with the trauma and memory of this event that took her mother's life.

First in 1993 at the World Trade Center, next in 1995 in Oklahoma City, then in 1996 during the Olympics, and finally in 2001 at the World Trade Center again. Americans have now joined much of the rest of the world in facing the reality of terrorism. No longer is this cowardly evil confined to foreign countries. We have experienced a twenty-first-century "Day of Infamy"—and life in the United States has been altered forever. People will be suffering the aftermath of this horror for years.

Trauma

Trauma is the response to any event that shatters your world. It's more than a state of crisis. Trauma leaves you feeling unsafe—your place of refuge has been invaded.

Documentation of this condition goes back to the story of Job, who lost his family, farm, and health suddenly and by violent means (Job 1:13–2:8). David had several close (and no doubt traumatic) encounters with death that involved animals, soldiers, King Saul, and giants in his lifetime (1 Samuel 17:1-52; 18:10-11,27; 19:8). He also witnessed hand to hand combat and thousands of brutal murders by Israeli warfare. These events so affected David that his personality was changed and his family life altered. His daughter Tamar was raped by her half-brother (2 Samuel 13:10-15), his son Amnon was killed at the command of his other son, Absalom, who later also died a violent death (2 Samuel 13:28-29, 2 Samuel 18:9-15). The Bible also recounts other traumas. In Judges 19 we read about a gang rape. Jonah was shipwrecked and swallowed by a big fish (Jonah 1:15-17). Paul was beaten, imprisoned, and shipwrecked three times

(2 Corinthians 11:23-28). The experience of Christ on the cross was very traumatic to both Jesus and His disciples.

Trauma was noted in the Middle Ages and during the American Civil War. Shakespeare wrote about it in *Henry IV.* But it wasn't until World War I that the term *shell shock* was coined. Later it was called *war memories.* It came to the forefront after the Vietnam War and became known as Post-Traumatic Stress Disorder, or PTSD. It's also referred to as *aftershock.*

The word *trauma* comes from a Greek word that means "wound." It's a condition characterized by the phrase, "I just can't seem to get over it." This experience is not limited to those who have gone through a war. I've seen it in the father who saw his daughter fatally crushed in an accident years ago; women who were sexually abused as children or who experienced an abortion have experienced it. I've seen it in the paramedic, the chaplain, and the nurse, and also in the survivor of a robbery, traffic accident, or rape. Trauma touches those subjected to pressure or harassment in the workplace. I also saw it in the face of those impacted by the terrorist attack in New York City.

If you've ever been to a rodeo, you've probably seen a rider pursuing a steer. He guides his horse next to that galloping steer and at the precise moment leaps from his horse, grabs the steer's horns, and pulls it to a dusty halt. With the right amount of pressure at the right time, he literally throws that steer to the ground. When you experience trauma, you are thrown about like that steer. Your world turns wild, out of control, crazy.

What we used to see as a safe world is no longer safe. What we used to see as a predictable world is no longer predictable. Most people overestimate the likelihood that their lives are going to be relatively free from major crises or traumas, and they underestimate the possibility of negative events happening to them. Perhaps that's why we're so devastated and our core beliefs shaken when they do. What beliefs do you hold about life? What will happen to those beliefs if you experience trauma? Will they be tested? Will they survive the testing? It's important to ask yourself these questions *before* trauma enters your life.

If you've been feeling invulnerable and thinking *It can't happen to me,* trauma will not only wound you and shake your beliefs, it will also fill your life with fear. Invulnerability is an illusion. You didn't have to be a victim of the bombing in Oklahoma City or New York City to suddenly feel extremely vulnerable. Just viewing the continuing vivid pictures on TV or the still photographs in the paper were sufficient to take you from the role of spectator to participant in the trauma. We all ended up feeling *If it can happen there, it can happen here.*

You see it all the time on TV. Most newscasts carry several stories with trauma potential. We see snatches of the tragedy, usually with a scene of a memorial service, a few anguished words from a family member or victim, and then the scene quickly shifts to another tragedy. It may be the last we see or hear of it, and perhaps the last we think about it. But it's not over for those involved; it's just beginning. For some victims the trauma will go on for years. For others it will go on for as long as they live.

What Can Lead to Traumatization?

Perhaps you're asking the question that most people ask: "How widespread are traumatic events in our country? How many people are exposed to traumatic events, such as natural and technological disasters, accidents, crime, abuse, and war?"

We used to say 75 percent of the general population has been exposed to some event that meets the criteria for becoming a trauma in our country. Now it's even higher.

But the good news is that only about 25 percent of those exposed to such events become traumatized.[1]

Of course, you can experience a crisis and not end up traumatized. There are also people walking around today who think and feel that the state of trauma they are in is just the way life is meant to be lived. But it's not.

Even if you're not a traumatized person, someone you know may be. What you understand about trauma can enable you to be a healing, supportive influence in that person's life.

Physical trauma can affect a person in two ways. Obviously, some part of the body is impacted with such a powerful force that the body's natural protection, such as the skin or bones, can't prevent the injury, and the body's normal, natural healing capabilities can't mend the injury without some assistance.

Perhaps not as obvious is the emotional wounding caused by trauma. Your psyche can be so assaulted that your beliefs about yourself, your life, your will to grow, your spirit, your dignity, and your sense of security are all damaged. You end up feeling helpless. You can experience this to some degree in a crisis and still bounce back. In trauma you have difficulty bouncing back because you feel de-realization *(Is this really happening?)* and depersonalized. *(I don't know what I really stand for anymore)*.

Elie Wiesel, a Nobel Peace Prize recipient and a survivor of Auschwitz, was with his wife in a taxi in Manhattan when the first Trade Tower was hit on September 11, 2001. They went home and watched the events recounted on television. He said, "We watched the first pictures. They were both surreal and biblical: The flames, the vertical collapse, and the disappearance of the world's two proudest towers. Many of us were stunned into silence. Rarely have I felt such a failure of language."[2]

As the result of trauma, something happens in our brain that affects the way we process information. It affects how we interpret and store the event we've just experienced. In effect, it overrides our alarm system. Trauma has the power to disrupt how we process incoming information. When we can't handle the stress, we activate our survival techniques.[3]

Most of us aren't aware of what happens to our brain. There's an alarm portion of the brain that controls our behavior. When we've been traumatized, this alarm system becomes hypersensitive. It overreacts to normal stimuli. For example, it sees a large person and feels, *He's going to hurt me. Oh, no!*

But another part of the brain is analytical and *calms down* the emotional part of the brain—it analyzes things and puts things in perspective—*No, a large person isn't necessarily going to hurt me.*

It's as though the left side (the cognitive) and the right side (the emotional) of the brain are temporarily disconnected from one another. Usually our body, emotions, and thoughts are all connected. Trauma separates these from one another. We may have vivid graphic thoughts about what happened, but no emotion. Or we might experience intense emotions, but without the thoughts or actual memories. As one man said, "I feel like my brain was disrupted and one part is transmitting AM and the other FM. Sometimes there are holes in my memory like a slice was taken out. Other times I can't get those intrusive unwanted memories to stop. I want them evicted! I can't remember what I want to remember and I can't forget what I want erased." This struggle is familiar to those who undergo trauma.[4]

Are some of us more susceptible to being traumatized than others? If I am emotionally healthy, if I came from a "healthy home," if I'm a strong Christian, will I be immune to this disorder? No. We're all susceptible to trauma; we're all at risk. Your previous mental stability, race, gender, level of education, previous emotional disorders or lack of emotional disorders seem to make no difference, although your ability to handle life's ordinary stresses and your personally developed coping skills can help. But trauma can overwhelm any of us.

What does make a difference, more than anything else, is the intensity and degree of stress. Studies have identified 58 general vulnerability factors as contributing to a person becoming traumatized. But researchers are still puzzled about which responses assist a person in adapting best to a traumatic event.[5]

If you end up traumatized, it's *not* because of a defect in you. Your reactions are normal in response to an abnormal event. Your personality doesn't alter the outcome of experiencing trauma, but trauma *does* impact your personality. Yes, we do vary in our responses and our capacity for endurance. Some people have better coping skills than others. Those who have a strong faith in Jesus Christ and an accurate understanding of life through the Scriptures have more resources to help them cope. But for all of us there comes a point in time when our defenses are overrun.[6]

There's one last factor to consider. Those who are involved in natural catastrophes seem to experience shorter and less intense PTSD than those involved in man-made disasters. As mentioned earlier, if a natural disaster can be seen as an act of nature or God—*That's just life*—the survivors don't lose as much trust in others as do those involved in man-made disaster. Another word for a man-made disaster is *atrocity*. That's why Oklahoma City, Columbine, and New York City have impacted us so much. Also, those who experience one trauma usually recover more quickly than those who have experienced multiple traumas.[7]

The Causes of Trauma

What experiences create traumas in our lives? There are a multitude of events. As you read the following paragraphs, consider the people you know (including yourself) who may have experienced such natural catastrophes as earthquakes, fires, floods, hurricanes, tornadoes, volcanic eruptions, landslides, or life-threatening windstorms. I've been in threatening windstorms and have been jolted out of bed by earthquakes. As a teen, my family's lives were saved by our Collie barking and alerting us to a fire in our home. Thankfully, none of these events was severe enough to traumatize me.

Sometimes there are community or work-related disasters, such as a chemical spill or an explosion.

Trauma can occur in the survivors of a refugee or concentration camp.

Many people have become traumatized through sexual or physical assault, and some have gone through satanic ritual abuse. By the age of 18, 25 percent of girls have been sexually abused and 16 percent of boys. For some children, trauma is not Oklahoma City. It's going home at night.

Children who are physically mistreated by excessive beatings, spankings, confinement, or deprivation of food or medical care can be traumatized.

You can be traumatized by witnessing a death or serious injury in a car accident; by seeing a victim of violent crime beaten, raped, or killed; by being exposed to an uprising, riot, or war.

The murder of a close friend or family member is traumatic. Children, who have even less capability than adults to handle significant events in their lives, can be more easily damaged. At risk is any child who has witnessed the murder, suicide, rape, or beating of a family member, significant adult, or friend. The number of traumatized children who experience the aftermath of gang violence in our society is growing.

Many of the conditions mentioned so far pertain to being a witness. When it happens to you, it's even worse. The list of events is extensive.

Being a combatant, prisoner, or medic in war creates the potential for trauma. Anyone who has been burglarized, robbed, mugged, abducted, raped, kidnapped, terrorized, or injured in a vehicular accident experiences trauma. Any situation in which you feel that you or another family member could be killed or hurt gives you cause to experience trauma.

Those involved in the helping professions are open to trauma if they've been involved in just one of the following conditions:

- witnessed death and injury
- experienced a threat to their own safety and life
- made life-and-death decisions
- worked in high-stress conditions

This last condition includes long work hours and an unsafe environment.

Paramedics, rescue teams (the rescue workers in the burned-out hulk of the Federal Building in Oklahoma City, the divers searching for bodies underwater amidst the torn fuselage of TWA flight 800, and all the various personnel at Ground Zero in New York City) police officers, firefighters, and medical personnel—all are at risk.

My son-in-law, who is a firefighter, has experienced first- and second-degree burns fighting fires. He has witnessed numerous deaths and has had to make many significant, life-and-death decisions. Firefighters frequently operate on very little sleep and sometimes work 48-hour shifts.

If someone you know has experienced any of the above events, then you or that person has experienced trauma. This doesn't mean that PTSD or being traumatized is a result. But the *event* that leads to this problem has occurred.[8]

And keep in mind that sometimes what is traumatic to one person may not be to another.

The Effects of Trauma

Trauma has many effects. It shatters your beliefs and assumptions about life, challenges your belief that you have the ability to handle life, and tears apart your belief that the world is a just and orderly place to live.

Trauma leads to *silence—I don't have the words to describe it.*

Trauma leads to *isolation—No one seems to understand the experience I had.*

Trauma leads to *feelings of hopelessness—There was no way to stop what happened or the memories of what happened.*[9]

Your optimism begins to crumble. Even your rationality turns against you. Basically, rationality is good and necessary. In a trauma, however, it can turn against us. Robert Hicks, in his book, *Failure to Scream,* writes:

> When trauma hits, our rationality becomes a curse. We are not like animals that, after sniffing a dead carcass, can walk off with no apparent feelings of remorse, anger or regret. Humans are more complex. We are *Homo sapiens* (Latin for "thinking man"). We think about our tragedy, and our thinking can drive us crazy. The replay of the event, the flashbacks, even the smells, bring up reminders of the trauma. As rational beings we seek the rationale in the trauma. When none is found, the traumatic blow is heightened. The meaninglessness of the event can drive one into despair, compulsive activities, or addictive relationships, which are all possible quick fixes for the pain. All of these feelings illustrate the depth to which our rationality has

been attacked and how shattered our world
has become.[10]

We all want a reason for what happens to us. We want to
know *why* so that we can once again have a sense of order
and predictability about life. But sometimes we must live
our lives with unanswered questions.

If you believe in a morality that says, "Right will always
prevail, and so will justice," what do you do when traumatic
events that seem unfair creep into your life? What do you do
when you expect the good guys to always win and the bad
guys to always lose, and it doesn't turn out that way?

You won't be the first or the last to cry out against injus-
tice. Listen to Job:

> If I cry out concerning wrong, I am not heard.
> If I cry aloud, there is no justice.
>
> JOB 19:7 NKJV

We want answers, we expect answers, we plead for
answers, but sometimes heaven remains silent. That's when
our faith undergoes a crisis in addition to whatever else is
impacting us. Perhaps you end up asking along with C.S.
Lewis,

> Where is God? This is one of the most dis-
> quieting symptoms. When you are happy, so
> happy that you have no sense of needing
> Him, so happy that you are tempted to feel
> His claims upon you as an interruption, if
> you remember yourself *and* turn to Him *with*
> gratitude and praise, you will be—or so it
> feels—welcomed with open arms. But go to
> Him when your need is desperate, when all
> other help is vain, and what do you find? A
> door slammed in your face, and the sound of

> bolting and double bolting on the inside.
> After that, silence. You may as well turn away.
> The longer you wait, the more emphatic the
> silence will become. There are no lights in
> the windows. It might be an empty house.
> Was it ever inhabited? It seemed so once. And
> that seemingly was as strong as this. What can
> this mean? Why is He so present a com-
> mander in our time of prosperity and so very
> absent a help in time of trouble?[11]

Trauma also affects how we see ourselves; it affects our self-identity. We all have a picture of ourselves. We may see ourselves as rational, strong, take-charge, in-control people. A trauma can change all that.

Traumatized persons often *re-experience the trauma.* Thoughts, pictures, dreams, nightmares, or even flashbacks of what occurred may take up residence in your life. Sometimes they slip into your mind like a video stuck on continuous replay. This sensitivity can become so extreme that an event can trigger a flashback and make you feel and act as if you were experiencing the original trauma all over again.

One fireman said, "After the Trade Tower disaster I heard about others who died, and it was like a carousel of faces running in front of me. There were classic pictures that will be in my head forever. I knew 30 guys that aren't here anymore. I can see them, feel them, taste them. I don't know what to make of it! There's just no language to describe what you see and feel. It's like a nightmare you can't wake up from. I see a lot of destruction, but this was magnified a million times. I'm just trying to grab onto life."

A friend of mine who is a Vietnam vet often experiences this at police funerals as he sees the flag-draped coffin. I've been with those who can't watch certain movies on TV because of the effect it has on them. I've been with a person who, when the loud rumbling of a truck goes by, reacted as though it was a major earthquake hitting again, similar to the one that traumatized him.

A combat veteran walks down a street and hears a car backfire. He dives behind a tree to hide from the enemy and recalls the memories of his friends who were blown up in front of him. A victim of rape or sexual abuse has a flashback when making love to his or her spouse. An accident victim has a flashback at the sight of a car wreck or blood. Someone sees an object falling from a building and once again he sees people jumping to their deaths from the World Trade Center.

Reminders, or triggers, can include the anniversary of the event. As the date draws near, the intensity of the actual trauma can build. Holidays and other family events can create strong emotional responses. It's possible for a traumatized person to be set off by something they see, hear, smell, or taste. In the case of abuse, a confrontation with the abuser may bring back emotional or physical reactions associated with the abuse.

Even the system that is designed to help the victim can cause a person to relive the painful event. It could be the court system, the police, the mental health system, or the sentencing process. Certainly the media doesn't help in their graphic descriptions of the worst incidents in life, nor do movies in their extensive portrayal of violence. These portrayals can bring back the memories of a traumatized person's victimization.[12]

In a flashback it's as though you leave the present and travel back in time to the original event. It seems so real. You see it, hear it, and smell it. Sometimes a person begins to react as if he or she were there. Many times a person is hesitant to admit this to others for fear of their reaction. A flashback is like a cry of something that needs to come out and does so in the only way it knows how. When survivors can talk about the trauma, write about it, and bring it to God in a very honest and real way through worship, there isn't as great a need for this memory to be so intrusive in nightmares, images, or flashbacks.

Sometimes a person re-experiences trauma not through memories or images but through *painful and angry feelings* that seem to come out of nowhere. These feelings occur because they were repressed at an earlier time. Now the emotions are simply crying out for release. This state reminds me of the poem by C.S. Lewis:

> Out of the wound we pluck the shrapnel
> Thorns we squeeze out of the hand.
> Even poison forth we suck, and after the pain we ease.
>
> But images that grow within the soul have life
> Like cancer often cut, live on below the deepest of the knife
> Wanting their time to shoot at some defenseless hour
> Their poison, unimpaired, at the heart's root
>
> And, like a golden shower, unanswerably sweet,
> Bright with returning guilt, fatally in moment's time
> Defeat our brazen towers long-built;
>
> And all our former pain and all our surgeon's care
> Is lost, and all the unbearable (in vain borne once)
> Is still to bear.[13]

Perhaps you or someone you know has experienced what Lewis has described. Many have but do not realize the significance of what they are experiencing.

Another way people re-experience trauma is through *numbing and avoidance*. It's painful to re-experience trauma. For some, it's agonizing. They want it to go away and disappear forever, but it doesn't. And so the body and the mind take over to protect against the pain. This is done by emotional numbing. Our defense system kicks into gear to help us adjust. When numbing occurs it can create a diminished interest in all areas of life. You could feel detached from others around you, even the ones you love the most. Often there is no emotional expression because you've shut down everything. You tend to reduce your involvement with life.[14]

When you re-experience trauma, sometimes you end up feeling some of the emotion you didn't experience at the time of the event because of the numbing that took place. Now when feelings of rage, anger, guilt, anxiety, fear, or sadness emerge you wonder, *Where did these come from? They hurt! I don't want them!* You shut down again so you won't feel as if you're going through a series of out-of-control mood swings. And then you begin to avoid situations you feel may trigger this condition. You retreat from other people, from family, and even from life. You do this mentally, socially, physically, and often spiritually.

You find yourself staying away from places where the problem occurred. If a person was robbed in a restaurant, he or she may avoid restaurants. Firefighters, police officers, and medical personnel may seek another line of work. A friend of mine was a counselor for a group of hospice nurses and patients. He told me they had lost 45 people in one year who were terminally ill. He said for his own sanity he was going into another profession. It had become too much for him to handle.

People who have experienced trauma have their own set of triggers that can activate the memories of what they experienced. The effort to avoid these situations can make a person a prisoner as well as create difficulty in interpersonal relationships.

Another characteristic of trauma involves a person's *increased alertness, usually referred to as hyperalertness or hyperarousal.* The strong emotions you experience—fear, anxiety, anger—affect your body, particularly your adrenaline output.

When people say they are pumped up, it's usually because of an adrenaline rush that puts the body into a state of hyperalertness. Adrenaline increases blood pressure, heart rate, muscle tension, blood-sugar level, and pupil dilation. Because the blood flow decreases to your arms and legs and increases to your trunk and head, you can think and move better. There's a name for this condition: "fight or flight." The fight occurs because of the increase of adrenaline. But if even more adrenaline pumps in, you freeze. You move and think in slow motion. Everything shuts down.

This condition is often evident through symptoms such as difficulty sleeping, periods of irritability for unknown reasons, difficulty concentrating, anxiety over crowds, and being easily startled.[15]

During a traumatic event, your heart begins to race, breathing is difficult, and muscles tighten. You may label these responses as catastrophic! Some, in their attempt to make sense of what is happening to them, mislabel their bodily responses. They say, "I'm going crazy," "I'm going to collapse," "I'm going to have a heart attack," or "I'm dying." Some never correctly relabel these bodily responses. So anytime their heart pounds or it's hard to breathe, they misinterpret what is happening and end up with a panic attack.[16]

For some victims of trauma, *emotions—such as fear—rage out of control like a river bursting through a dam.* I work with many people who are paralyzed by fear. Sometimes they fear making a decision, risking another's disapproval, or taking a stand. They may fear that other people don't like them. And even worse, they fear breaking out of this pattern they are trapped in. Others are paralyzed in some other way by their trauma.

Physical paralysis is a terrible thing. To be locked up— immobilized— so that your body can't function and respond to the messages of your mind is frustrating. But it is even more frustrating when the paralysis is the limitation or immobilization of the mind.

Scripture tells us about a man who was paralyzed in his mind (his emotions) as well as in his body:

> After these things there was a feast of the Jews, and Jesus went up to Jerusalem. Now there is in Jerusalem by the sheep gate a pool, which is called in Hebrew Bethesda, having five porticos. In these lay a multitude of those who were sick, blind, lame, and withered... And a man was there who had been ill for thirty-eight years. When Jesus saw him lying there, and knew that he had already been a long time in that condition, He said to him, "Do you wish to get well?" The sick man answered Him, "Sir, I have no man to put me into the pool when the water is stirred up, but while I am coming, another steps down before me." Jesus said to him, "Get up, pick up your pallet and walk." Immediately the man became well, and picked up his pallet and began to walk.
>
> JOHN 5:1-9

The man in this account had been paralyzed for 38 years. He lay by the pool day after day, waiting for a way to be free of his affliction. Beneath this famous pool, which was actually deep enough for people to swim in, was a subterranean stream. Every now and then the stream bubbled up and disturbed the waters of the pool. The Jewish people believed that this disturbance was caused by an angel, and the first person to get into the pool while it was bubbling would be healed from any illness.

When Jesus discovered the lame man by the pool, He asked him one of the strangest questions in all of Scripture: "Do you want to be healed?" Or to put it another way, "Do you want to change?" I suppose the man was rather taken aback by Jesus' seemingly unsympathetic question. Didn't Jesus understand that he had been brought to this pool day after day, week after week, year after year for healing? Didn't Jesus understand that he had asked person after person to help him get into the pool?

Or could it be that Jesus asked the question because He knew what was really going on inside this man? It's possible that after so many years of frustration and paralysis the man's helplessness had turned into hopelessness. Perhaps all hope for healing had died, and in its place was a dull despair. His answer seems to indicate this, for instead of just replying yes, he gave as an answer the reason why he could not be healed. He would go through the motions each day of trying to get into the pool, but in his heart perhaps he believed that he would never touch the water.

Many who have been traumatized feel the same way. The intensity and duration of their symptoms seem to close the door to recovery.

Three Stages of Recovery

This chapter on trauma is basic and overly simplified. The information is meant to alert you to the fact that trauma exists and is perhaps closer to you than you realize. If you identify yourself as one of those experiencing any degree of PTSD, or you know someone who fits the characteristics, remember this:

1. *Being traumatized is not incurable. Recovery is possible,* but it is a slow process.

2. *You will need to work with a professional,* someone who is equipped to assist those experiencing trauma.

This could include a highly trained minister, chaplain, or therapist.

3. *You can promote healing through understanding.* The more you learn about trauma for yourself or for others, the more you will feel in control of your life.

There is another side to trauma. The current research on those traumatized indicates the majority of victims say they eventually benefited from the trauma in some way. And these are people who experienced as much pain as those who didn't fully recover. How did they benefit? There was a change of values, a greater appreciation for life, a deepening of spiritual beliefs, a feeling of greater strength and appreciation and building relationships.

The most important element in recovering is to remain connected to other people.[17]

Aphrodite Matsakis, author of *I Can't Get Over It: A Handbook for Trauma Survivors*, has done extensive research work with those suffering from PTSD. She takes a very positive approach to the healing process. She explains that for healing to occur you need to stop seeing yourself as a person who is diseased or deficient. You are not abnormal because of your trauma symptoms; it is the event or events that you experienced that are abnormal. The event was so out of the ordinary that it overwhelmed you, as it would anyone.[18]

There are three stages in trauma recovery: the *cognitive* stage, the *emotional* stage, and the *mastery* stage. The cognitive or thinking stage, involves fully facing your trauma, remembering it, and even reconstructing it mentally. This isn't a matter of dwelling in the past, but of taking fragmented and disconnected memories and pulling them together so that you can make sense of the present. Sometimes this stage involves talking with others, recreating the scene, or reading written accounts of it. When this is accomplished you will then be able to view what happened from a new perspective—an objective view rather than a judgmental view.[19]

In the cognitive stage you need to look at what happened to you as a detached observer (even though it may be difficult) rather than as an emotionally involved participant. If you're able to work through this stage, you will acquire a new assessment of what your real choices were during your traumatic experience. You will have a better understanding of how the event has impacted the totality of your life and you will be able to reduce the self-blame that most of us experience. Finally, you will gain a clearer understanding of who or what you are angry at.[20]

The cognitive stage deals with the mental area, but healing and recovery must also involve the *emotional* level. This second stage will necessitate dealing with any of the feelings you repressed in any way because of the trauma. You must experience those emotions at the gut level. This can be difficult, because many people have a fear of feeling even worse and losing control. You don't have to act on the feelings, nor will they take over your life. But you do need to face them. These emotions could include anger, anxiety, grief, fear, sadness…the list goes on and on.[21]

The final stage is the mastery stage. This is when you find new meaning through what you have experienced, your perspective becomes that of a survivor, rather than a victim. A person who has a relationship with Jesus Christ and a biblical worldview has the greatest potential to become a survivor.

Mastering the trauma involves making your own decisions instead of allowing experiences, memories, or other people to make decisions for you. This is a time of growth, change, and new direction in your life. What you learn because of a trauma, you probably could not have learned any other way. Look at what Scripture says about this:

> Blessed be the God and Father of our Lord Jesus Christ, the Father of mercies and God of all comfort; who comforts us in all our affliction with the comfort with which we ourselves are comforted by God. For just as the sufferings of Christ are ours in abundance, so also our comfort is abundant through Christ. But if we are afflicted, it is for your comfort and salvation; or if we are comforted, it is for your comfort, which is effective in the patient enduring of the same sufferings which we also suffer.
>
> 2 CORINTHIANS 1:3-6

I've had people ask me, "How do I know I'm growing and getting better?" First, you have to develop a new way of looking at progress. It may be slow. There may be regressions. You need to focus on the improvements rather than the times you feel stuck. One man told me that he rated his progress each month on a scale of one to ten, as well as his entire journey of healing up to that point. That helped him understand his own progress.

How can you tell if you're progressing and moving ahead? Your symptoms become less frequent, and the fear you struggled with will become less intense. One of the fears that is so disheartening is the fear of going crazy or insane. This fear will also diminish.

Anger and grief, which exist hand in hand, will lessen. What remains can be directed into positive directions. Candy Lightner, whose daughter was killed by a drunk driver, founded Mothers Against Drunk Driving (MADD). A friend of mine, traumatized by the Vietnam War, spends time each week using his energy to help the men in our local veterans hospital. He and his Alaskan husky take the men to worship services and other activities. He's taught his dog to talk—people words! I've heard him, and it's amazing. He and his dog provide a great deal of entertainment and laughter. Writing letters—contacting congressmen and state senators in a properly assertive, consistent manner—is another positive activity that can bring about change.

However, there will be times when the only way to get rid of your anger and feelings of revenge is to face the fact that you can't do anything to change what happened to you or prevent a similar occurrence in the future. Then begin to give up a portion of your anger or resentment each day. One victim said,

> I finally realized that holding on to my anger kept me victimized. As much as I wanted someone to pay, I knew it wouldn't happen. So I decided on a 90-day plan. I would allow myself to keep 10 percent of my anger since I know I'm human and won't be perfect. But each day for 90 days I would give up 1 percent of my anger. The fact that I had a goal and then developed a plan really encouraged my recovery. Each day I spent 15 to 20 minutes identifying who or what I wanted to avenge. I wrote it out each time and then put it in the form of a brief letter. I stood in a room and read it out loud unedited. Sometimes it wasn't pretty. And sometimes I read it to a friend because it helped having a live body there.
>
> Each day I wrote the phrase "I forgive you for..." and then put down the first reason I could think of for not forgiving. It was like I was full of rebuttals against forgiving. I would

> always end the morning by reading a praise psalm out loud. Then I would lift my hands to the Lord and give Him my anger for the day. Then I thanked Him for what He was doing, even if I didn't feel like it. I discovered many things through this: I was full of bitterness. It kept me pinned down and stuck. I didn't want to forgive. They didn't deserve it.
>
> But I kept at it. I wondered after 30 days if I'd made even 3 percent improvement. But by the time 60 days were over I felt ahead of schedule. I was improving; I was growing; I got well. Sometimes the anger and grief still hit me. I can live with that even if it's a companion the rest of my life. I have days and weeks when I feel whole again. Praise God for this.

Taking positive steps like this will help you make the shift from victim to survivor. *Believing* that you can become a survivor will accelerate this process.

As you move through your journey to recovery, the rigidity that helps you to cope will diminish. You will gradually discover the value of flexibility and spontaneity to the degree that you are comfortable with it, based upon your own unique personality type.

One of the delights of recovery is developing a new appreciation of life. You begin to see what you weren't seeing before, to hear what you couldn't hear before, to taste what was tasteless before.

Some people rediscover their sense of humor and all its healing properties.

You will discover a new and deeper sense of empathy for the wounded around you. You actually become a wounded healer and have greater compassion for others.

Romans 12:15, which says, "Weep with those who weep," takes on a new meaning.[22]

People who are recovering commonly struggle to see and measure their progress. For years I've had people keep a daily or weekly journal in which they explicitly write out what they are experiencing or feeling. Some keep a time line of recovery. Some do both. Over time this makes a person aware, in a tangible way, of his or her recovery.

A recovery time line (see diagram, see page 171) is a simple way to record the peaks and valleys of the recovery process. Plot the days on the bottom and a scale of 1 to 10 on the left. At the end of each day, indicate where you are for that day. This might go on for months or years, but over time you will discover that you are growing.

When you've experienced trauma, sometimes that's all you remember. What would happen if you were able to leapfrog over that event back to what your life was like before the trauma? We call this "looking at your life as it was." What was your life like? What did you do each day? Answer the following questions to help you remember life before the trauma:

- What was your biggest struggle then?

- What fulfilled you?

- What did you enjoy the most?

- What did you look like then? (It helps to be very specific about this. Sometimes pictures and videos help the process.)

- Who were your friends?

- What did you like and not like about yourself?

- Who did you get along with?

- Who didn't you get along with?

- What did you believe about God then?

- What were your Christian practices, such as prayer?

- What were your beliefs about life then?

- What were you realistic about? Naïve about?

- What did you want out of life then?

- What were your goals or dreams for yourself then?

- What are your goals or dreams for yourself now?

- What would you like to be different now?

As you look at what you write, what specifically is different now? What alternatives can you come up with to make your life more the way you want it to be? Make a list of all the things you would like to happen now (dream big), and then check off what possibly could happen if you choose to pursue this avenue. What would keep you from growing and changing? For many, it's the lack of a plan. Dreams can fade without a plan. Perhaps someone else could help you with this part of the exercise.

Overcoming trauma is a process—a journey. But you don't travel the journey alone; the Lord is with you.

> The Spirit of the Sovereign Lord is on me,
>   because the Lord has anointed me
>   to preach good news to the poor.
> He has sent me to bind up the brokenhearted,
>   to proclaim freedom for the captives
>   and release for the prisoners.
>
> ISAIAH 61:1 NIV

When Jesus spoke again to the people, he said, "I am the light of the world. Whoever

follows me will never walk in darkness, but
will have the light of life."

JOHN 8:12 NIV

You, O Lord, keep my lamp burning;
    my God turns my darkness into light.

PSALM 18:28 NIV

Days

Recovery

"God, Are You There?"

Finding God in the Midst of Suffering

God, where are You?
(Silence)
God, I'm looking for You. Where are You?
(Silence)
God... I want to know. Where are You?
(Silence)
God...why don't You answer me?
(Silence)

God, why are You so still? Don't You care? How could You let this happen? You know what I'm talking about. Were You in Lockerbie, Scotland, when the airplane blew up? Where were You when that mother pushed her car into the lake and drowned her two sons? Were You there when that couple, who waited 12 years for a baby, buried him at 15 months of age? Were You in Bosnia when a whole ethnic group was slaughtered? Where were

You, God, when Oklahoma City happened? Were You there? Why did all those innocent children have to die? What about Columbine? Were You in New York City and the Pentagon and the field in Pennsylvania?

> O Lord, how long must I call for help before you will listen? I shout to you in vain; there is no answer. "Help! Murder!" I cry, but no one comes to save. Must I forever see this sin and sadness all around me?
>
> HABAKKUK 1:2-3 TLB

> Should you be silent while the wicked destroy those who are better than they?
>
> HABAKKUK 1:13 TLB

> God...*are You there?*...You're *not* there—
> You're gone. I knew it. I'm abandoned.
> (Silence)
> God...if You're there, all I want to know is...
> why? Give me a reason. Why? Why? Why?

The psalmist cried out the same way we do:

> Lord, hear my prayer! Listen to my plea! Don't turn away from me in this time of my distress. Bend down your ear and give me speedy answers, for my days disappear like smoke. My health is broken, and my heart is sick; it is trampled like grass and is withered. My food is tasteless, and I have lost my appetite. I am reduced to skin and bones because of all my groaning and despair. I am like a vulture in a far-off wilderness, or like

an owl alone in the desert. I lie awake, lonely as a solitary sparrow on the roof.

My enemies taunt me day after day and curse at me. I eat ashes instead of bread. My tears run down into my drink because of your anger against me, because of your wrath. For you have rejected me and thrown me out. My life is passing swiftly as the evening shadows.

PSALM 102:1-11 TLB

Too often what we hear when we ask why, is nothing—nothing at all. Why? Why? Why? The sound of silence can be deafening. Sometimes this silence comes just before something bad happens. Or right after, like the oppressive stillness when two cars finally roll to a stop after a collision heard blocks away.

As a child you heard the silence of a parent or teacher who just stared at you after discovering your involvement in something you weren't supposed to be doing! Or you're in a major business meeting and you speak out and contradict the chairman of the board, which no one ever does, and the silence (and the glares) are louder than thunder. Or you sit in the doctor's office and hear the silence of the doctor before he tells you a difficult-to-hear diagnosis.

Nothing makes you feel more rejected than the silence of a spouse who refuses to talk with you. You feel disconnected, separated.

Often silence is the prelude to something devastating. Revelation 8:1 NIV says: "When he opened the seventh seal, there was silence in heaven for about half an hour."

When there is silence, you feel isolated, all by yourself, alone. As Habakkuk the prophet cried out to God, so did the psalmist.

How long, O Lord? Will you forget me forever?
How long will you hide your face from me?

PSALM 13:1 NIV

My soul thirsts for God, the living God.
When can I go and meet with God?
My tears have been my
food day and night,
While men say to me all day long,
"Where is your God?"

PSALM 42:2-3 NIV

I say to God my Rock,
"Why have you forgotten me?
Why must I go about mourning,
oppressed by the enemy?"

PSALM 42:9 NIV

We want answers because suffering rarely makes sense. We want answers because suffering causes us to wage war with our beliefs. Often the biggest problem we struggle with is what we believe about problems. Dr. Lloyd Ogilvie suggests,

> First of all, we believe that problems including crisis, losses and anything that doesn't go our way is bad for us. Whatever disrupts the flow of our life and is unpleasant or causes distress can't in any way be beneficial for us. Problems are a bother, an invasion, a disruption and they have no real benefit.
>
> We also believe in entitlement. We deserve to live a problem-free life, especially if we're

faithful, diligent, hard-working and plan ahead.

The third belief has to do with God. If we believe in Him, serve Him, follow His Word, He will (or ought to) make sure our life runs without any difficulty. We believe that God owes us clear sailing in life.[1]

So where is God during a crisis? He may not seem anywhere near. And if God isn't around and we can't count on Him, what hope do we have? That's the way many feel.

A pastor, Gary Kinnaman, describes what we experience:

> I am sure you understand that when I speak of the absence of God, I am talking about a *sense* of absence. God is *always* present with us—we know that theologically—but there are times when he withdraws our consciousness of his presence.
>
> In all honesty these theological niceties are of little help to us when we enter the Sahara of the heart. This is where we experience real spiritual desolation. We *feel* abandoned by friends, spouse, and God. Every hope evaporates the moment we reach for it. Every dream dies the moment we try to realize it. We question, we doubt, we struggle. Nothing helps. We pray and the words seem empty. We turn to the Bible and find it meaningless. We turn to music and it fails to move us. We seek the fellowship of other Christians and discover only backbiting, selfishness, and egoism.[2]

The biblical metaphor for these experiences of forsaken-ness is the desert. It is an apt image, for we do indeed feel dry, barren, parched. With the psalmist we cry out,

> O my God, I cry out by day, but you do not
>   answer,
> by night, and am not silent.
>
> PSALM 22:2 NIV

In fact, we begin to wonder if there's a God to answer us.

These experiences of abandonment and desertion come to us all. How then, can we get beyond feeling abandoned? How can we know for certain that God is there with us in the midst of our suffering?

A man who struggled with cancer for 20 years wrote to a friend two years before he died:

> The despair of the sufferer is not caused by the depth of the suffering but by the depth of his sense of separation from God.
>
> You said that when you were finally able to get hold of God, the peace came. The suffering didn't diminish, it was as deep as ever, but the sense of separation had vanished. You no longer felt separated from God.[3]

Called to Suffer

The source for what we believe has to be the Word of God. When we look at it, we discover that time and time again Scripture tells us that God is *good,* and He is concerned for mankind. Scripture also tells us that God is omnipotent. That means He is all-powerful. But what does all-powerful mean to you? Sometimes we look at it incorrectly. Does all-powerful mean that we are robots, and He causes every single thing that happens in the world? It's true that He is all-powerful, but that doesn't necessarily mean everything that happens in the world is the way He wants it.

At the creation of the world, God created mankind with the ability to make choices. Sometimes man's choices result in things that are not what God desires. God could not give us the freedom to love Him if we didn't also have the freedom to reject Him and His teachings. He wants us to love Him based upon our own choice. As Dr. Dwight Carlson suggests,

> It is further possible that since God greatly desires individuals who willingly love, worship and follow Him, He had no alternative but to allow Satan to test them with pain, suffering and misfortune. This is one of the major points taught in the Book of Job. Let me assure you that this does not mean God is not sovereign; in the Book of Job, Satan had to request permission to test Job, and God allowed it only within very fixed limits (Job 2:6).
>
> Recognition of God's self-imposed limitations is the most difficult concept to grasp. Many ardent Christians will have difficulty with this viewpoint. But I am convinced that when God created the world, He set laws in motion which even He chooses to honor. The problem for us is that these laws intersect our lives in the most sensitive areas—in our suffering and our misfortune. This leads to an interesting question: Who is at the center of this universe—God or us? In his book *When Bad Things Happen to Good People*, Harold Kushner asks:

> "If God can't make my sickness go away, what good is He? Who needs Him? God does not want you to be sick or crippled. He didn't make you have this problem and He doesn't want you to go on having it, but He can't make it go away. That is something which is too hard for even God. What good is He, then?"[4]

This question raised by Kushner seems to reflect the idea that we are the center of the universe and God is there to do our bidding. But C.S. Lewis has a different perspective.

> Man is not at the center. God does not exist for the sake of man. Man does not exist for his own sake.[5]

What it boils down to in this life is that you and I have been called to suffer. Suffering is inevitable.

There is another kind of suffering to which we've been called—suffering with others. And it begins first with Jesus. "If children, then heirs, heirs of God and fellow heirs with Christ, provided we *suffer with him*" (Romans 8:17 RSV, emphasis added). Jesus doesn't ask us to avoid suffering. He expects us to choose to suffer with Him. Why? Consider these reasons:

> [God] comforts us in all our troubles, so that we can comfort those in any trouble with the comfort we ourselves have received from God...Indeed, in our hearts we felt the sentence of death. But this happened that we might not rely on ourselves but on God, who raises the dead...On him we have set our hope that he will continue to deliver us, as

you help us by your prayers. Then many will give thanks on our behalf for the gracious favor granted us in answer to the prayers of many.

2 Corinthians 1:4,9-11

Daniel Simundson, in *Where Is God in Our Suffering?* reminds us that:

> When we cry out to God in our times of suffering, we know that we will be heard by one who truly knows what we have gone through. It is a great comfort for a sufferer to know that presence of an understanding and compassionate God, who not only invites our very human prayers but also knows what it is like to be in so much pain. God hears. God understands. God suffers with us. The lament is heard by One who has been there.[6]

God allows suffering so that we can enter into another person's sorrow and affliction. Joyce and I have experienced this numerous times as couples have sought us out either because they have a disabled child or have lost a child in death. Because we have already walked the path they are now walking, they want to talk with us.

When you experience a crisis in your life, you will have compassion and understanding for others going through the same experience. As we read in 2 Corinthians 1:11, suffering gives us the opportunity to learn to give thanks in every situation and event of life. Notice that I said "the opportunity to learn." You may not be there yet. That's all right. You'll be there someday.

Lewis Smedes puts a different light on this idea in his book, *How Can It Be All Right When Everything Is All Wrong?* (Isn't that an honest title?)

Put it as plainly as it can be put: we need to suffer some of the cussed wrongness of life in order to find its deep righteousness. We have to feel pain we do not want to feel, carry burdens we do not want to carry, put up with misery we do not want to put up with, cry tears we do not want to shed. If we feel no hurt now, we will, when all is done, be the most miserable of all people. Ultimately, at the end of the game, when we cash in our chips, it will be all right with us only if we have been hurt with life's wrongness.[7]

He suggests that there are two ways to suffer. We can suffer *from* something and we can suffer *with* someone.

We suffer from something when pain comes to us, grabs us in its claws, crushes us, unwilling, captive.

Suffering with someone does not hurt any less than suffering from something. The difference is not in the amount. The difference lies only in the will. In suffering from something, we simply receive it, nobly or meanly, with heroic courage or ordinary cowardice, but we do not choose it. In suffering with somebody, we take it into our own hands to suffer. We choose to do what we do not have to do, or even want to do; we walk, eyes open, into the pain of another human being and claim it as our own.[8]

That is our calling as believers. If you are married, you will have the opportunity to suffer with your spouse. If you are a parent, you will suffer with your children. You put yourself into the shoes of the other person, you experience their pain, their hurt, their agony, their burdens. It's called empathy, and it *hurts*. But it also has a healing quality.

We need to remember that in life, pain is inevitable, but misery is optional. We cannot avoid pain, but we can avoid misery. God has given us such immense freedom that He will allow us to be as miserable or as joyful as we want to be.

Called to Joy

I know some people who spend their entire lives practicing being unhappy, diligently pursuing joylessness. They get more mileage from having people feel sorry for them than from choosing to live out their lives in the context of joy.

Joy is simple (not to be confused with easy). At any moment in life we have at least two options, and one of them is to choose an attitude of gratitude, a posture of grace, a commitment to joy. Peter said,

> Dear friends, do not be surprised at the painful trial you are suffering, as though something strange were happening to you. But rejoice that you participate in the sufferings of Christ, so that you may be overjoyed when his glory is revealed.

1 PETER 4:12-13

Which words leap out at you in those verses? You probably noticed the words *troubled, trials,* and *suffering*. But remember, not only was suffering mentioned, joy was mentioned as well.

Recently I saw the musical presentation of Victor Hugo's *Les Miserables*. It's the story of grace. It's also the story of a man, Jean Valjean, who receives an unjust sentence for stealing a loaf of bread. He tries to escape and ends up spending 19 years in jail. Both his sentence and suffering were unjust. But he also lived in an unjust world. As a result of what he experienced he became very bitter. This only intensified as he discovered what it was like to be an ex-convict in nineteenth-century France. He was constantly rejected. In time, this experience would embitter most people.

One night Valjean was so desperate that he looked for a place to stay at the home of a Catholic bishop. But Valjean took advantage of the bishop's kindness. During the night he stole most of the bishop's silver. Once again, however, he was unsuccessful in his thievery. As he tried to leave, the police caught him and took him back to the bishop's house. Much to their surprise, the bishop handed two silver candlesticks to Valjean saying, "You forgot these," implying to the police that the silver was a gift.

When the police left, the bishop looked at Valjean and said, "I have bought your soul for God." And in the bishop's merciful act of claiming Valjean for God, Valjean's bitterness left him.

The rest of Victor Hugo's novel shows what happens when a life is redeemed. If anyone had a reason to hate and lash out it was Valjean. Instead, he followed the bishop's example of mercy. He raised an orphan given to him by her mother as she was dying. He spared the life of the parole officer who spent years tracking him down. He saved his future son-in-law from death, even though he was almost killed in the process. He lived out the rest of his life with a sense of joy, returning good for evil.

Here was a miserable, embittered man struggling with suffering that he never deserved. But he also had another experience that was undeserved—the grace and mercy he received at the hand of the bishop.[9]

The author of *A Grace Disguised* sums it up this way:

His suffering was undeserved, but so was his redemption.

Like Valjean, I would prefer to take my chances living in a universe in which I get what I do not deserve—again, either way. That means that I will suffer loss, as I already have, but it also means I will receive mercy. Life will end up being far worse than it would have otherwise been; it will also end up being far better. I will have to endure the bad I do not deserve; I will also get the good I do not deserve. I dread experiencing undeserved pain, but it is worth it to me if I can also experience undeserved grace.

So, God spare us a life of fairness! To live in a world with grace is better by far than to live in a world of absolute fairness. A fair world may make life nice for us, but only as nice as we are. We may get what we deserve, but I wonder how much that is and whether or not we would really be satisfied. A world with grace will give us more than we deserve. It will give us life, even in our suffering.[10]

When We Can't Help Asking Why

When we suffer, at first we spend our energy trying to discover who or what caused our hurt and pain. In fact, most of us spend our energy trying to figure out the cause before deciding what to do with it. The more we expend our energy there, the less energy we have available to work on what to do!

Suffering and pain always produce something. Paul writes in 2 Corinthians 1:9 that pain turns us to God. The suffering produces something—we are changed.

This is *not* a grin-and bear-it attitude. Nor are you to act as if nothing has happened. You are *not* in denial. It doesn't mean that you act happy and delighted about a crisis when your heart is torn apart and you feel like weeping. And it doesn't say to rejoice or be glad *immediately!* As Philip Yancey puts it:

> The Bible's spotlight is on the end result, the use God can make of suffering in our lives. Before He can produce the result, however, He first needs our commitment of trust in Him, and the process of giving Him that commitment can be described as rejoicing.[11]

Isn't it interesting that on the one hand we allow ourselves to be dependent upon Him, yet on the other hand we sabotage the comfort He would bring to us by making Him into a villain?

It's easy to lay the responsibility for life's tragedies upon God. Dr. Dwight Carlson writes:

> The belief that God is in control of the universe leads some people to conclude He has planned every last detail and wants every event to come about exactly as it does. Such a God would delight in pushing misfortune buttons: this God says, "Let's give Mary an F on her English test today. Let's give Joanne a dent in her fender. I'll clog up Pat's sink. Joe will get a heart attack, and I'll give Susan leukemia." Nothing could be further from the truth.[12]

The other side of blaming God is believing that we are special because of our relationship with Him or because we have done something for Him, and therefore He will insulate us from the misfortunes of life.

> God might intervene—at His sovereign choosing—but it is not our divine right to demand His intervention.[13]

The problem is not with asking why; the problem is with arguing with God, demanding that He defer to our desires and do it our way. If He did that, we would have created our own God.

So, we're back to the question: Why? It's a lingering question when you're in crisis. It's one you grapple with and put to bed. Then about 2:00 A.M. it jumps up and runs around again. At first, asking why is not really a question that seeks an answer. No answer would suffice, even if it were given by God. In fact, if God answered, we would probably argue with Him.

The word *why* is used again and again in the Psalms. It's a cry against that which has invaded our lives. It is a cry of protest as well as a lament. One writer said:

> It places the issue of human suffering before and in front of God. It is to ask why, for what reason, to what end, does [He] remain silent? It also assumes that this suffering is unjust.[14]

Have you ever wondered what makes you keep asking this question? I mean, most of the time a part of us realizes that we won't really find an answer. But today's generation has the attitude, "We have a right to know." We need "full disclosure" of what's going on and why it's going on. Asking why in relationships tends to put people on the defensive, because it often has an accusatory tone or implication.

When our lives have been disturbed, we seem to need an answer to retrieve the orderliness we crave—there must be some logical reason for what has happened. Because most people like order, answers, and certainty, they are sometimes quick to give us glib, trite, theological answers when we're in a crisis. An unanswered "Why?" threatens the other person's security! If it happened to us, then why not to them? Perhaps this is why Job's friends responded to him as they did. And we, like Job, end up saying,

> So how can you console me with your nonsense?
> Nothing is left of your answers but falsehood!
> JOB 21:34 NIV

Another reason we pursue answers is to prevent the crisis from occurring again.

Perhaps we also ask in order to look outside of ourselves to diffuse our own sense of shame. We ask why to quiet the inward voice that says, *What was my responsibility in this? Could I have done more, done better, done something different so that it wouldn't have happened?* If we can find an answer outside of ourselves, we feel less guilty.

Often I think the "why" question is a way of blaming God—making Him responsible. But the real question should be "Why *not* me?"

I've had people ask why there is so much evil in the world. But as Scott Peck observes, I've not had anyone ever ask "Why is there good in our world?"[15] I've heard people blame God; rarely have I heard them blame Satan. They blame God, but rarely do they blame the consequences of original sin.

Don't get the idea that asking why is wrong. It's a normal human response when life begins to unravel. It's the first step along the way to more significant questions and discoveries. Unfortunately, some people never progress beyond why. They remain stuck with this question for years. They never discover that it is an unanswerable question—a step toward discovering the useful questions.

Nowhere does Scripture tell us *not* to ask God why. Paul wasn't reprimanded because he asked God three times to remove the "thorn in his flesh." God expects us to cry out when we plow through the dark and dangerous alleys of life. It's all right to ask God to remove the present adversity. Jesus also made such a request: "Going a little farther, he fell with his face to the ground and prayed, 'My father, if it is possible, may this cup be taken from me. Yet not as I will, but as you will'" (Matthew 26:39 NIV).

James 1:2-4 talks about our response to trials. Then we read in verse 5, "If any of you lacks wisdom, he should ask God, who gives generously to all without finding fault, and it will be given to him" (NIV).

James is saying that if you have any questions while you're going through these trials, go ahead and ask. When God believes that you need the answer to your question, He will give it to you.

Moving Beyond "Why?"

As Joyce and I cared for our retarded son, Matthew, over a period of time we began to ask questions. The questions will vary for each person, but our questions took this form:

"What can we learn through this experience?"

"How can we grow through this?"

"How can God be glorified through this?"

There are no timetables or deadlines for getting beyond the why question. New questions cannot be forced, nor should they be forced upon anyone. It's a matter of growth. And asking new questions does not depend upon the original problem being resolved. Sometimes you find yourself returning to the why question, even as you ask others. This, too, is normal.

The new questions are broader in focus and include other people. "Why?" merely focuses on self. The questions beyond why are growth questions that can prevent us from becoming stuck in the past and present. They open the door to the future.[16]

God is not obligated to explain Himself to us. Sometimes we don't have the ability to understand the reasons for a crisis, or it is impossible for us to grasp the entire picture. In several places Scripture mentions that this is the way life is:

> It is the glory of God to conceal a matter.
>
> PROVERBS 25:2 NIV

> The secret things belong to the LORD our God.
>
> DEUTERONOMY 29:29 NKJV

> As you do not know the path of the wind,
>   or how the body is formed in a mother's
>   womb,
> so you cannot understand the work of God,
>   the Maker of all things.
>
> ECCLESIASTES 11:5 NIV

> "For my thoughts are not your thoughts,
>   neither are your ways my ways," declares
> the LORD.
> "As the heavens are higher than the earth,
>   so are my ways higher than your ways
>   and my thoughts than your thoughts."
>
> ISAIAH 55:8-9 NIV

We are people who usually put faith in formulas. We feel comfortable with predictability, regularity, assurance. We want God to be this way too, and so we try to create Him in the image of what we want Him to be and what we want Him to do.

However, you and I cannot predict what God will do. Paul reminds us of that in Romans 11:33 NKJV: "Oh, the depth of the riches both of the wisdom and knowledge of God!

How unsearchable are His judgments and His ways past finding out!"

God is not uncaring or busy elsewhere.

He is neither insensitive nor punitive.

He is supreme, sovereign, and loving.

Is God in control? Yes! But He's in control with infinite wisdom.

God is the absolute sovereign of the universe, but He has given us freedom. He created us to love Him, but there could be no mature love between us and Him without our freedom to choose.

I don't fully comprehend God. I, too, have unanswered questions about some of the events of my life. But all of life's trials, problems, crises, and suffering occur by divine permission. As Don Baker wrote:

> God allows us to suffer. This may be the only solution to the problem that we will ever receive. Nothing can touch the Christian without having first received permission of God. If I do not accept that statement, then I really do not believe that God is sovereign—and if I do not believe in His sovereignty, then I am helpless before all the forces of heaven and hell.[17]

God allows suffering for His purposes and for His reasons. This should help us to see God as the gracious Controller of the universe. God is free to do as He desires, and He doesn't have to give us explanations or share His reasons. He doesn't owe us. He's already given us His Son and His Holy Spirit to strengthen and guide us.

We look at problems and losses and ask, "Why?" Jesus asks us to look at these events and ask, "Why not?" What God allows us to experience is for our growth. Just as God has arranged the seasons of nature to produce growth, He arranges the experiences of the seasons of our lives for growth. Some days bring sunshine and some bring storms. Both elements are necessary.

God knows the amount of pressure we can handle. First Corinthians 10:13 tells us that He will "not let you be tempted beyond what you can bear" (NIV). But He does let us be tempted, feel pain, and experience suffering. He doesn't always give us what we think we need or want; He gives us what will produce growth.

When we ask God, "Where are You?" we may come to realize that He is always there in the midst of the crisis. But we still can't help but ask Him, "When will You answer?" Just as David cried,

> How long, O Lord? Will you forget me forever?
> How long will you hide your face from me?
> How long must I wrestle with my thoughts
> and every day have sorrow in my heart?
> How long will my enemy triumph over me?
>
> Psalm 13:1-2 NIV

We want Him to act according to our timetable. Scripture says, "Be still before the Lord and wait patiently for him" (Psalm 37:7 NIV). To block out the pain of waiting, we are often driven to frantic activity. This does not help, but resting before the Lord does:

> Often waiting is a time of darkening clouds. Our skies do not lighten. Instead, everything seems to become even more grim.
>
> Yet the darkening of our skies may forecast the dawn. It is in the gathering folds of deepening shadows that God's hidden work for us takes place. The present, no matter how painful, is of utmost importance. Somewhere, where our eyes cannot see and our

ears are unable to hear, God is. And God is
at work.[18]

You may not feel that God is doing anything to help you
recover. Why? Because you want recovery *now*. The quick-
fix mentality of our society often evokes a distorted perspective of God. We complain about waiting a few weeks or
days, but to God a day is a thousand years and a thousand
years is a day. God works in hidden ways, even when you
and I are totally frustrated by His apparent lack of response.
We are merely unaware that He is active. Hear the words of
Isaiah for people then and now:

> Since ancient times no one has heard,
>   no ear has perceived,
> no eye has seen any God besides you,
>   who acts on behalf of those who wait for him.
> You come to the help of those who gladly do right,
>   who remember your ways.
>
> ISAIAH 64:4-5 NIV

God has a reason for everything He does and a timetable
for when He does it.

> "For I know the plans I have for you,"
> declares the LORD, "plans to prosper you and
> not to harm you, plans to give you hope and
> a future."
>
> JEREMIAH 29:11 NIV

Give yourself permission not to know the what, how, and
when of your circumstances. Even though you feel adrift on
a turbulent ocean, God is holding you and knows the direction of your drift. Giving yourself permission to wait can
give you hope. It is right for God to ask us to wait for weeks
and months and even years. During that time, when we do

not receive the answer and solution we think we need, He gives us His presence.

> But I trust in you, O LORD;
>   I say, "You are my God."
> My times are in your hands.
>
> PSALM 31:14-15 NIV

Philip Yancey concludes his book *Where Is God When It Hurts?* with these words:

> So, where is God when it hurts?
>
> He has been there from the beginning, designing a pain system that still, in the midst of a fallen, rebellious world, bears the stamp of His genius and equips us for life on this planet.
>
> He has watched us reflect His image, carving out great works of art, launching mighty adventures, living on this earth in a mixture of pain and pleasure when the two so closely coalesce they sometimes become almost indistinguishable.
>
> He has used pain, even in its grossest forms, to teach us, asking us to let it turn us to Him. He has stooped to conquer.
>
> He has watched this rebellious planet live on, mercifully allowing the human project to continue its self-guided way.
>
> He has let us cry out and echo Job with louder and harsher fits of anger against Him, blaming Him for a world we spoiled.
>
> He has allied Himself with the poor and suffering, establishing a kingdom tilted in their favor, which the rich and powerful often shun.

He has promised supernatural strength to nourish our spirit, even if our physical suffering goes unrelieved.

He has joined us. He has hurt and bled and cried and suffered. He has dignified for all time those who suffer by sharing their pain.

He is with us now, ministering to us through His Spirit and through members of His body who are commissioned to bear us up and relieve our suffering for the sake of the head.

He is waiting, gathering the armies of good. One day He will unleash them. The world will see one last explosion of pain before the full victory is ushered in. Then, He will create for us a new, incredible world. And pain shall be no more.[19]

Listen, I tell you a mystery: We will not all sleep, but we will all be changed—in a flash, in the twinkling of an eye, at the last trumpet. For the trumpet will sound, the dead will be raised imperishable, and we will be changed. For the perishable must clothe itself with the imperishable, and the mortal with immortality. When the perishable has been clothed with the imperishable, and the mortal with immortality, then the saying that is written will come true: "Death has been swallowed up in victory."

"Where, O death, is your victory?
Where, O death, is your sting?"

1 CORINTHIANS 15:51-55 NIV

Survivors, Part 1

How Do They Do It?

There are times when crisis hits that you feel like a parakeet I heard about. Everything was going along well for this little bird. His life was smooth with all his needs met, until that fateful morning. One minute he was sitting on his perch and the next he was tumbling end over end and down a narrow tube until he fell into a pile of dirt and dust. You see, his owner had decided to clean the cage. So, she got out the vacuum cleaner, removed the attachment from the end of the hose, and stuck the hose into the cage. Just then the phone rang. Distracted by the phone, she lost her grip on the hose and it settled on the bird. Away he went.

Realizing what she had done, the bird owner dropped the phone, turned off the vacuum, and fearfully opened the bag. The parakeet was alive, but stunned and filthy. She grabbed the bird, ran to the bathroom, turned on the large faucet in the bathtub, and proceeded to hold him under the water. Then she realized that her bird was gasping for air, as well as shivering. So she reached for her hair dryer, put it on high, and hot air blasted him.

The parakeet? He never knew what hit him. Oh, he lived, but he never sang much after that. He just sort of sat and stared.[1] His life had been changed by an unexpected crisis.

Change is inevitable when a crisis invades your life.

What Comes After the Crisis?

Crisis and change go hand in hand. The question is, "Do you want to be a victim of change, or do you want to take charge and determine the direction it takes you?" Everyone has a choice when a crisis hits. The definition of a survivor is a person (or family) who gets knocked down—but then gets up and works *through* the crisis. The nonsurvivor just gets back in the ring and gets clobbered all over again.

If you've already experienced a crisis, you know what I'm saying. Some couples and families draw closer together and become more compassionate during a crisis. Others become splintered and soon disintegrate. Some individuals stagnate while others grow, even as they carry wounds and scars.

Many families, instead of working out solutions for their pain and problems, begin to attack each other in the months following a crisis, whether the event is the birth of a disabled child, the discovery of a child's disability, a child's rebellion, a family member's death, a job loss, or some other traumatic change. If conflicts have been buried for years, a crisis lifts the restraints, and old conflicts erupt with a new source of fuel. Now the family has to deal not only with the crisis itself but also with other unresolved conflicts. Each drains energy needed to cope with the other.

A family works together like a large body. Each person is an integral part of the body. When the body loses an arm (as in a death), is permanently injured (as in a disabled father), or one part refuses to cooperate with the rest and instead does its own thing (as in a rebellious child), all the other parts are affected. They have to learn to adjust. Sometimes they assume new roles.

It's similar to balancing an old-fashioned balance scale. If something is added to one side it alters the other side by the same amount in the opposite direction. If the scale is ever to be balanced again, something has to be added to one side or subtracted from the other.

Your family life is like that scale. If a crisis tips the scales in one direction, the family members have to adjust to handle the change and get back into balance. Many aspects of family life—including power, responsibilities, and roles—may need to be reassigned. The longer the central individual in the crisis was in the family or the greater the significance of his or her position (such as the oldest child rebelling), the more adjustments will need to be made.

I've seen cases in which one child committed serious offenses that drew attention away from the parents' marriage problems. When the child was jailed and no longer there, the marriage problems became apparent, and another child became the troublemaker to ease the marital tensions. In some families, when a parent leaves or loses a job, other issues that have gone unnoticed begin to surface.

Between the time a crisis occurs and the individual family members discover their new roles and begin to stabilize, there's a time of uncertainty and turmoil. Because of the reality of the loss, it's difficult to make some of the necessary changes. Each family member needs time and space to deal with the crisis in his or her own way. It may take a while for each one to find a new role. A person feels like a juggler at times, trying to deal with his or her own needs and still be helpful to the other family members.

After a crisis hits, you'll also have to weigh the needs of a particular family member against the needs of the family as a whole. You'll have to work to achieve a balance. What do you do, for example, when a child dies or runs away close to Christmas? How do you respond when some of the family wants to get a Christmas tree and celebrate Christmas as usual, and some don't?

How do people survive crisis? How do families survive? Must a person have a certain type of background or upbringing to be a survivor when a crisis hits? Consider this:

> In 1962 a fascinating report *Cradles of Eminence* was published by Victor & Mildred Goertzel. They studied 413 famous and exceptionally gifted people to learn what produced such lives. The results were not quite what a person might expect. About 80 percent of the later famous children hated school. Seven out of ten of the group came out of homes full of trauma and dysfunctions, including absentee parents, conflictual parents, poverty and a variety of physical handicaps. But almost every single handicap and difficulty had been overcome so they could become all they were meant to be.[2]

Choosing How to Handle Change

Families and individuals who cope well with heartbreak and crisis have specific characteristics, as do those who don't handle crisis well.

What sets survivors apart from nonsurvivors? There are things we can learn from the wisdom and experience of those who make it. Dr. William Mitchell suggests that nonsurvivors follow what he calls path A.

They *curse* the crisis. They add to the negative situation by adding a negative opinion. They actually compound the negativity.

They also *nurse* the crisis. Their time and attention is centered on the problem rather than on looking for a solution.

Finally, they spend their time *rehearsing* the problem. In their minds they replay it again and again until it dominates their every waking moment.

There is, however, a path B—the path survivors take. They *disperse* the crisis. One of the most effective ways of handling minor and major difficulties is to take what seems to be an overwhelming problem, break it down into smaller parts, and then tackle each smaller part one at a time.

John was injured in an accident that was clearly the other driver's fault. He was incapacitated for almost a year, during which time he lost his job. After six months, disability payments ran out. The other driver was uninsured, and John's insurance was such that it barely kept pace with his medical costs. There were so many unfair aspects to his situation that it would have been easy for John to focus on the unfairness and place blame. For a brief time (one day) John and his family allowed themselves to do just that. Then they said (and these are their exact words), "We can gripe and sit on the pity pot, or we can be survivors—what will it be?"

They decided to become pioneers and carry out a new lifestyle until Dad was well enough to work. The family spent a week brainstorming how they could make do with what they had, cutting costs to the bare minimum. They thought of ingenious and creative ways to make money and identified which friends and family members they could ask for whatever help they needed.

Since John had to stay home, he found some ways to make money through various jobs. He also called the pastoral staff at his church to see what he could do to assist them during this time. Each week the family allowed themselves a "one-hour family gripe time" when they could dump all their feelings and complaints. Often this time turned into laughter as they learned to be "creatively ridiculous" in their griping. But they always ended their session with a time of listing their blessings and what they had to be thankful for. They concluded with a time of thankful prayers. This family not only survived a crisis, they grew through it!

Survivors *reverse* what they can about the crisis, just like John's family. This doesn't mean you can make a crisis disappear. But you can look for some glimmer of hope, some ray of light. You can choose to be problem oriented or you can choose to be solution oriented. You can choose not to dwell on the negative. Once again, the difference between a nonsurvivor and a survivor is in the way the person thinks about the crisis. Scripture has much to say about this.

> Have this attitude in yourselves which was also in Christ Jesus.
>
> PHILIPPIANS 2:5

> Now your attitudes and thoughts must all be constantly changing for the better.
>
> EPHESIANS 4:23 TLB

> Fix your thoughts on what is true and good and right. Think about things that are pure and lovely, and dwell on the fine, good things in others. Think about all you can praise God for and be glad about it.
>
> PHILIPPIANS 4:8 TLB

> So watch what you do and what you think.
>
> JAMES 2:12 TLB

Let's take a more in-depth look at what makes the difference between survivors and nonsurvivors.

What Defines a Survivor?

Survivors Plan Ahead

Survivors tend to *plan ahead* in order to effectively handle the transitions of life. Losses and crises will come as unwelcome guests into every life. Survivors anticipate the possibility of future problems and make plans to handle what may happen. They make plans for coping, and they stick to their plans. They are realistic when they hear about a crisis. They are able to think about and discuss the question, "How would I (or we) handle a situation like this?"

Have you anticipated some of the difficulties you will face in the next few years? It could be anything from an unexpected move, a business failure, a death in the family, a child leaving home early, or an adult child returning home. Do you have a plan for handling these "surprises"? What will you do?

One family shared with me that diabetes ran through the husband's side of the family. At the time he and three of his siblings already had diabetes and were on insulin. Two of his siblings were not doing well, since they chose a path of denial over the years rather than face the fact that diabetes might hit them.

This family was already educating their children about the characteristics of the disease and its warning signs. The family kept abreast of the newest treatments as well as preventive approaches. They carefully watched their diets, as this can be a major factor in the disease.

I've seen more and more individuals—before they are hit with a crisis—attend classes on "Handling Stress and the Crises of Life." These are people who want to prepare themselves.

Joyce and I live in an area plagued by fires, floods, and earthquakes. A number of our friends lost just about everything in the Northridge earthquake several years ago. My mother's four houses and the home in which I was raised in the Hollywood Hills were almost destroyed by a raging fire in the late '70s, which burned 25 homes around us. So the possibilities of disasters are very real.

Joyce took a "Community Disaster Training" course and participated in a simulated earthquake recovery drill. She keeps her identification vest and hard hat at hand in the closet. We also carry earthquake survival kits in each car. That's being prepared!

Individuals and families who don't do well are *not prepared* for life's setbacks. They survive well when things are going well. Some actually deny the possibility that a crisis could happen to them. When other people experience divorce, death, unemployment, or illness, they seldom feel any empathy. I've actually talked with people attending my "Recovering from the Losses of Life" seminars who have difficulty identifying any major crisis in their lives.

One man said, "Norm, I just can't relate to any of these experiences people are describing. What does that say about me? Is this a problem in my life?"

I asked, "How would you handle it if you experienced some major crisis or tragedy? What would you do?"

He paused for a moment and then said, "I don't know. I've never thought about it. I guess I never thought it would happen to me."

Unfortunately, too many people believe crisis only happens to others.

Survivors Cultivate a Biblical Attitude

Some crises you know you will experience in life, but other crises take you totally by surprise.

There have been many events in or near my life that I never anticipated would happen. I never expected that an office next to mine would be blown up by terrorists, with people injured and killed. But it happened.

I never expected a business associate to mismanage the running of my business to the extent that I would almost lose that business. But it happened.

I never expected that a high school boy on one of my outings as a youth director would fall over a 400-foot cliff to his death. It happened. I watched as they carried him out in a body bag on a horse.

I never expected that my daughter at the age of 20 would take a detour in her Christian life and live with boyfriends, use cocaine, and move into alcoholism. But it happened, and continued for four years.

I never expected to have my only son born profoundly mentally retarded with brain damage and then suddenly die at the age of 22. But it happened.

Over the years my wife and I have learned the truth and significance of many passages from God's Word. One passage in particular came alive as we depended on it more and more: "Consider it all joy, my brethren, when you encounter various trials, knowing that the testing [or trying] of your faith produces endurance" (James 1:2-3).

The Amplified version says, "But let endurance and steadfastness and patience have full play and do a thorough work, so that you may be [people] perfectly and fully developed [with no defects], lacking in nothing" (James 1:4).

Learning to put that attitude into practice is a process. The passage does not say, "respond this way immediately." You have to feel the pain and grief first, and then you'll be able to consider it all joy.

What does the word *consider* mean? As I studied in commentaries, I discovered that it refers to an internal attitude of the heart or mind that allows the trial and circumstances of life to affect us either adversely or beneficially. Another way James 1:2 might be translated is this: "Make up your mind to regard adversity as something to welcome or be glad about."

You have the power to decide what your attitude will be. You can say about a trial, "That's terrible. Totally upsetting. That's the last thing I wanted for my life. Why did it have to happen now? Why me?"

The other way of "considering" the same difficulty is to say, "It's not what I wanted or expected, but it's here. There are going to be some difficult times, but how can I make the best of them?" Don't deny the pain or hurt you might have to go through, but ask, "What can I learn from it? How can I grow through this? How can I use it for God's glory?"

The verb tense used in the word *consider* indicates a decisiveness of action. It's not an attitude of resignation—*Well, I'll just give up. I'm stuck with this problem. That's the way life is.* If you resign yourself, you will sit back and do nothing. But James 1:2 indicates you will have to go against your natural inclination to see the trial as a positive. There will be some moments when you'll have to remind yourself, *I think there's a better way of responding to this. Lord, I really want You to help me see it from a different perspective.* Then your mind will shift to a more constructive response. This often takes a lot of work on your part. Discovering the truth of the verse in James and many other passages like it will enable you to develop a biblical perspective on life. And that is the ultimate survival tool. Notice it doesn't say this is an immediate response. It takes time. The greater the loss, the worse the trauma, the longer our recovery will take.

God created us with both the capacity and the freedom to determine how we respond to the unexpected incidents life brings our way. You wish that a certain event had never occurred, but you can't change the fact that it did. The key word here is *attitude*. You can choose which attitude you will have! Listen to the story of one woman.

> The day had started out rotten. I overslept and was late for work. Everything that happened at the office contributed to my nervous

frenzy. By the time I reached the bus stop for my homeward trip, my stomach was one big knot.

As usual, the bus was late, and jammed. I had to stand in the aisle. As the lurching vehicle pulled me in all directions, my gloom deepened.

Then I heard a deep voice from up front boom, "Beautiful day, isn't it?" Because of the crowd I could not see that man, but I could hear him as he continued to comment on the spring scenery, calling attention to each approaching landmark. This church. That park. This cemetery. That firehouse. Soon all the passengers were gazing out the windows. The man's enthusiasm was so contagious I found myself smiling for the first time that day.

We reached my stop. Maneuvering toward the door, I got a look at our "guide": a plump figure with a black beard, wearing dark glasses and carrying a thin white cane. Incredible! He was blind!

I stepped off the bus, and suddenly all my built-up tensions drained away. God in His wisdom had sent a blind man to help me see—to see that though there are times when things go wrong, when all seems dark and dreary, it is still a beautiful world. Humming a tune, I raced up the steps to my apartment. I couldn't wait to greet my husband with "Beautiful day, isn't it?"

Source Unknown

As Dr. Joy Joffe puts it, "What happened to you was truly horrible. But you have a choice. You can live the rest of your life as a memorial service or you can put it away and get on with it."[3]

The 1952 Olympics were special to a young Hungarian boy. He stood in front of a target and because of his perfect right hand and eye coordination hit the target time after time. He won a gold medal in shooting for himself and for Hungary. Six months later he lost his right arm. Four years later the Olympics were in Melbourne, Australia. He was there. This time he used his left hand and he hit the bull's-eye again and again. He won another gold medal. He made a choice not to be limited by his limitations.

One of the best ways to clarify our response to what we can't understand, can't explain, or do not like is set forth in a phrase by Dr. Gerald Mann. He suggests that we are "free to determine what happens to what happens to us." Did you catch that? It's a choice.[4]

When I was a child in the 1940s, I saw the Disney movie *Dumbo, the Flying Elephant*. I've discovered that most people, no matter what their age, have viewed that film, thanks to video. Do you remember the story? Dumbo was a young circus elephant but a bit different from the others. He was born with huge ears. And so the other elephants thought he was weird—a freak. The only one who didn't make fun of him, naturally, was his loving mother.

Dumbo did have his difficulties. His ears were so big that he could hardly walk without tripping on them. And he seemed to get into all sorts of trouble because of those ears. He wished he hadn't been born with this problem.

But he did have one friend. A small circus mouse felt sorry for him. He encouraged Dumbo to just ignore what others said about him and look at himself as someone special. But it didn't seem to matter what Dumbo did—things just kept going downhill for him.

There was one scene in the film that was a turning point for Dumbo. One morning he woke and discovered that he and his mouse friend were high up in a tree nestled in the branches. They couldn't imagine how they had gotten up there. I mean, have you ever seen an elephant climb a tree? They were puzzled, and after talking about it, concluded that somehow Dumbo must have flown up into the tree.

At this point in the film the little mouse said, "Dumbo, you can fly!" But it was his next statement that was so insightful. He looked at Dumbo and said, "The very things that held you down are going to carry you up and up and up."

What Dumbo initially saw as something terrible, a deformity, a limitation, became something valued. His ears didn't change—his perspective did. He found the good in what seemed to be bad.

Survivors Learn from Others

When it isn't possible to plan ahead, survivors *learn from others* who have gone through difficult times in life. Do you know someone who has survived difficulties and grown through the experience? It may be someone you know personally or someone you've read about like Joni Eareckson Tada, who is paralyzed, or Dave Dravecky, the major league baseball player whose pitching arm was amputated in 1991 because of cancer.

In the book *Charlie's Victory*, the story is told of 30-year-old Charlie Wedemeyer, a high school coach who was told by the doctor that he had ALS, commonly known as Lou Gehrig's disease. It's a progressive, debilitating, paralyzing disease. He was given one year to live. But for the next seven years he continued to coach.

When he could no longer walk, his wife Lucy drove him up and down the sidelines in a golf cart. In time, he couldn't talk anymore, so she read his lips and passed on his instructions to the players. In his last season, after he had gone on round-the-clock life support, his team still won the state championship.

How did this man survive so long? How did this marriage stay intact? They focused on what they had together rather than what they were missing. Lucy said,

> I think we communicate and understand each other better today than we ever did. While I've learned to read Charlie's lips, I find I often don't have to. His eyes almost always tell me exactly how he feels, and his eyebrows punctuate those feelings as they bounce up and down or his forehead furrows into a wrinkle. And if you don't think someone in difficult circumstances can find happiness and contentment, if you doubt the contagious quality of joy, well, you've never seen Charlie smile.[5]

Their commitment of love to one another made them survivors.

I have learned so much over the years in working with others in order to help them. The reality is, they help me to grow.

Survivors Express Negative Emotions in Healthy Ways

Survivors find healthy ways to *express hurt, anger,* and *resentment.* They don't bottle up their hurt feelings, nor do they complain and force their discomfort on others. They talk, they share, and they cry. Oh, how they cry! Tears are God's gift, especially at times like these.

When words fail, tears are the messenger. Tears are God's gift to all of us to release our feelings. When Jesus arrived in Bethany following the death of Lazarus, He wept (John 11:35). And so will we. Ken Gire describes the value of tears.

> The closest communion with God comes, I believe, through the sacrament of tears. Just

as grapes are crushed to make wine and grain to make bread so the elements of this sacrament come from the crushing experiences of life.

And sometimes the crushing starts early.

One day your dog doesn't come home and you go calling for it. Another day passes, and you go looking for it. And on the third day when you're looking for it, you find its stiff body on the side of a well-trafficked street, and you bundle it up, carry it off, dig a hole in the backyard, and you bury it with a rock as a tombstone and tears as a eulogy.

Or someone at school dies from cerebral hemorrhage, or several someones in a sudden car wreck.

Or someone you've fallen in love with hasn't fallen in love with you, and you think life can't go on.

Or you learn from the orthopedic doctor that you can no longer play the sport you have loved for half of your still very young life, and maybe it's not the thing that should bring tears, but it does.

Or a grandparent dies. A grandparent who loved you and teased you and hugged you and brought "a little something for you" every time she came to visit. And now there's a freshly dug hole in the backyard of your heart.

Or a parent dies, and now the whole backyard is one big hole.

Or a marriage ends between two people you thought would be the last to break up, and besides the grief you feel, you sense the mortar of life loosening a little and the unsettling feeling that if it could happen to

them, it could happen to anyone, even to
you...[6]

In a newer book, *From My Own Tears,* I
have learned that if you follow your tears,
you will find your heart. If you find your
heart, you will find what is dear to God. And
if you find what is dear to God, you will find
the answers to how you should live your life.[7]

When our tears come, instead of feeling bad for shedding
them, or apologizing for them, we can remember their value.

When you don't admit your feelings, they become con-
cealed and withheld. Bottled-up feelings lead to bitterness,
vulnerability, and distorted perceptions. Chaplain Robert
Hicks says that in disasters those who are crying or
screaming will be better off than those who sit quietly, passive, unable to let it out.

The blows of life hurt us. But often those
who hurt most are silent. The screamers are
better off than their silent counterparts. At
least they know they are hurt and feeling
their pain. For various reasons, we don't
allow ourselves to experience the pain we
feel. Often others are to blame.

They don't want to hear about our pain,
or it makes them feel uncomfortable about
their own failure to scream, or perhaps it just
makes them feel awkward. Therefore, the
pain ends up being covered with work,
alcohol, sex, drugs, depression, compulsive
eating, dieting, and the endless list of acting
out behaviors that indicate to alert observers
that all is not well. Having failed to scream
they are now screaming through their disorders, addictions, and compulsions. To scream
is normal when facing tragic events. Not to

> scream may reveal the extent to which we
> are bleeding to death on the inside.[8]

Don't listen to those who say you shouldn't let your feelings out.

Deferring the necessary noise of grief should be seen as a warning cry for an individual or a family in crisis. Unfortunately, men especially have a tendency to "go it silently alone."

Over the years, we've found that families who have difficulty coping, frequently hurt one another by keeping silent. Interaction among family members is vital. Often, however, they retreat into their own inner worlds and don't express their thoughts or feelings. Sometimes some family members want to talk but others don't. The family may not communicate at critical times because they never learned to talk when everything was going well. People aren't likely to have the energy, time, and capability to learn communication skills when life is falling apart around them.

Survivors Live in Community

Most people don't realize that a silent person has power over other family members. For those who want to talk, the silence adds to the pressure of the crisis, and they end up feeling rejected and isolated. *Survivors do not live independently.* They have learned to draw on their own strengths and gifts and use them effectively, yet they still ask for and can accept assistance from others. They can also express concern and warmth to others. Silence is a characteristic of dysfunctional families; it destroys and deadens hope. And as the silence progresses, estrangement and frustration increase.

Survivors Look for Solutions

Survivors concentrate more on *solutions* than on blame.

Blame is one of the most significant characteristics of individuals and families who *don't* make it. None of us likes being out of control and left hanging. There has to be some closure to discovering what created the problem in the first place. If we have an explanation for what happened, we can understand it better, handle it better, and feel relieved that someone else was at fault. The more serious the crisis, the greater we feel the need to discover the cause. Statements that start with the words "If only you had (or hadn't)…" or "Why didn't you (or did you)…" begin to fly between one person and another. If a family member knows the other person's areas of vulnerability, the accusations can get vicious.

You may not want to blame others. You know that blaming doesn't make sense. But good sense doesn't often prevail after a crisis. Rather, the surge of emotional turmoil and the struggle for a reason for the difficulty become uppermost. When you blame, you create a war zone, and the other side retaliates.

Because everyone is vulnerable at this time, accusations and other comments penetrate deep into the mind and heart of the receiver and will be remembered for years. No one wants to be unfairly accused or blamed.

In Proverbs we read, "There are those who speak rashly, like the piercing of a sword" (12:18 AMP), and "In a multitude of words transgression is not lacking" (10:19 AMP). These verses clearly reflect the pain of unfair accusation.

Perhaps it's time for you to stop and reflect on the character-istics of survivors described in this chapter. The principles stated here are helpful not just for the crisis times of life but for everyday living.

What about it? Are survivor characteristics a part of your life right now? If not, don't despair; they can be. You can follow others who have learned the steps to becoming a survivor. Like so much else in life, it's a choice. You *can* make that choice!

Survivors, Part 2

How Do They Do It?

Recovering from crisis—the ability to bounce back from life's traumas—this is what you've been reading about in this book. Some of the chapters may have been uncomfortable for you to read. That's understandable. They may have brought up memories you wish had remained buried. But recovery is not about dredging up the pain of the past; it's about equipping you for the present as well as the future.

This book is a survival guide. That's why we're looking at the characteristics of those who have survived. We can learn from the experiences of others. As you have read about some of these people, hopefully you've started to consider how to make the principles of surviving a crisis a vital part of your life. This chapter will give you even more principles.

Survivors Face Reality

Those who survive *face what has happened to them*. They don't run, avoid, or deny. They name what has happened to them and face the devastation it has created. Eventually they learn to accept the existence of the crisis and its fallout in their lives and go with it instead of resisting it.

You have to face the seriousness of your crisis and the magnitude of what you have lost. You need to feel it to the depths of your soul and talk about it again and again. Sometimes people immerse themselves in a bundle of activities to avoid the pain. Activity doesn't make the pain go away. It just intensifies it.

Survivors affirm what they have lost. Going to a gravesite and placing flowers is a simple way to acknowledge your loss. Joyce and I do this several times a year. Five of our family gravesites are in close proximity—Joyce's father, mother, and brother; our son Matthew, and my mother.

Our country has tried to help the survivors of the Vietnam War recover by creating the Vietnam Veterans Memorial in Washington, D.C. The memorial is only visible when you walk into the grounds of the Constitutional Gardens. The piece of polished black granite starts with just one name. Then the granite grows taller and taller with row upon row of names on it—58,022 of them. The black wall helps us to remember what we've lost. It helps the viewer focus on sacrifice, bravery, friendship, and loyalty. It also helps to heal men and women's spirits.[1] There are memorials in Oklahoma City and there will be in New York City. We need these reminders of what we've lost.

Robert Veninga summed it up so gracefully when he said, "Once you have experienced the seriousness of your loss, you will be able to experience the wonder of being alive."[2]

From his vantage point on a cliff 75 feet above the ocean, Wayne Monbleau learned a valuable lesson from a seagull:

> I noticed a solitary seagull, slowly drifting
> toward me on the air currents.

In fact, quite a wind had kicked up. As it came in off the ocean, I could see the trees bending under its force. An occasional crow came scooting by, propelled forward by the strong breeze. All the while this seagull didn't seem to be moving a muscle. It just kept drifting toward me effortlessly.

Wait a minute! How could this gull be floating toward me when the wind was blowing against it? This seagull should have been riding the currents away from me, not toward me. What was happening here?

My attention became completely fixed on this bird. I noticed other gulls, furiously flapping their wings as they attempted to fly into the wind. It didn't work. One by one, they gave up. They would peel off to one side, and when the stiff breeze grabbed them, they were quickly whisked away out of sight. But this single gull I had been watching for a few minutes now just kept drifting on. How long had it been since this seagull had flapped its wings? How was it able to come toward me against the wind, while all the other birds had been exerting their full power and had failed?

As I sat there pondering these questions, I had an inner feeling that there was something important for me to see here. Then I felt the Spirit of God speak to my heart. Here is the gist of what I remember His inner voice saying to me that day: "The difference between this bird and all the other birds is that the others are fighting the wind, while this gull has learned how to submit itself to the wind. By yielding to its power, rather than resisting its power, this seagull has learned how to ride the wind. This bird has a different "attitude." Its body is positioned so that this contrary wind, which is beating back the others, is actually being used to propel this seagull forward. By passively accepting the breeze, this gull is going places where the others, with all their effort and straining, can never go.[3]

Survivors Don't Magnify Their Problem

Families who do not cope well often magnify the seriousness of their problems. They take them to the extreme and imagine the worst possible consequences instead of being hopeful or waiting to see what the actual results will be. They interact too much and in the wrong direction. When they discuss their crises only amongst themselves, without outside objective assistance, they easily become overly pessimistic. They're not solution-oriented but problem-centered. They often use the "victim phrases" that reflect a desire to just give up.

> "I can't..."
> "That's a problem..."
> "I'll never..."
> "That's awful!"
> "Why is life this way?"
> "If only..."
> "Life is a big struggle."
> "What will I do?"

We hear so much today about people being victimized by someone else. But there are more people who are victimized by their own beliefs and attitudes. By using victim phrases, we reinforce the control that problems or hurts exert over our lives. Every time we think or say one of these phrases, we subconsciously begin to believe it and fulfill it. Eventually we talk ourselves into believing these phrases represent the truth, and we become victims of our own beliefs.

Survivors may start out making these statements, but they learn to move from pessimism to optimism. They learn to challenge their victim thinking and come up with alternatives that will move them forward rather than keep them stuck.

"I can't." These words are prompted by three attitudes that often hinder us from moving on with our lives—the attitudes of unbelief, fear, and lack of hope.

When you say "I can't," you're saying that you have no control over your life. It's no harder to say, "It's worth a try." You'll like the results of this positive phrase much better.

"That's a problem." Those who see life's complications as problems or burdens are immersed in fear and hopelessness. Life is full of barriers and detours. But with every obstacle comes an opportunity to learn and grow if you hold the right attitude. Using other phrases, such as, "That's a challenge" or "That's an opportunity for learning something new" leaves the door open for moving ahead.

"I'll never..." This victim phrase is the anchor of personal stagnation. It's the signal of unconditional surrender to what exists or has happened in your life. It doesn't give a person or God an opportunity to work through the crisis. It's much better to say, "I've never considered that before," or "I haven't tried it, but I'm willing to try." This opens the door to personal growth.

"That's awful." Sometimes this phrase is appropriate in view of the shocking, dire situation we often hear about or

experience. In time we can learn to respond by saying, "Let's see what we can do about this situation," or "I wonder how I can help at this time," or "I wonder how I can do this differently."

"Why is life this way?" This is a normal response to the deep pains and sudden shocks of life. Some people experience one hurt and disappointment after another. Others experience a major setback and choose to linger in its crippling aftermath without recovering. They continue to use this victim question over and over again for months and years. They fail to make the transition to the "what" and "how" questions—what can I learn through this and how can God be glorified through this?

Remember that life is unpredictable and unfair. It isn't always the way we want it to be. But our response to life is our choice.

Joy in life is a choice. *Growth* in life is a choice. *Change* in life can be a choice. Choice comes before joy, growth, and change.

In the space of just one year, one woman experienced her husband's death, a daughter's divorce, and the other daughter's imprisonment. What was her response?

> When pain comes, it comes in piercing, specific jolts. That's what I felt when we received a phone call that Barbara had been arrested. The pain seemed to stay in the very pit of my stomach and never left for months. It seemed to just hit in different degrees with each event that took place after her arrest. I thought then that this is the worst thing that could ever happen. I began to wonder where God was in this intense pain that wouldn't stop hurting. I spent so much time trying to

figure out why we were all having to go through this before I decided how I would respond to this tragedy. I had a choice to either give up or face this head-on and trust God that He would see us through. I am glad I chose to trust my heavenly Father, because He has been faithful...

When the doctor sat across from my husband and me and told us my husband had Hodgkin's disease, the same intense pain hit me again. I thought, this is it, this was more than I could bear.

I was so afraid! Fear had taken over. How could I make it without Gary? How could I handle Barbara's situation? And Michael is only eleven years old; he needs a father. So for a year and a half I watched Gary dwindle away and each day the Lord gave me strength to take care of him and prepare me for the days ahead without him. God used all this pain in its grossest form to teach me to turn to Him and totally trust Him.

Knowing that He has hurt with me and cried with me and loved me through His Spirit and through members of His body has lifted me up. I can face tomorrow.[4]

Tim Hansel, who survived a fall in a mountain climbing accident and has been in pain for over 20 years, writes:

I've survived because I've discovered a new and different kind of joy that I never knew existed—a joy that can coexist with uncertainty and doubt, pain, confusion, and ambiguity. A journal entry a couple of years ago, written in the midst of the most trying period I've ever experienced, says simply, "I gave up looking for certainty—and found truth." I realized that when I quit waiting for certainty to come, I was free to discover, or rediscover, the essence of what I was really looking for.

Joy is a process, a journey—often muffled, sometimes detoured; a mystery in which we participate, not a product we can grasp. It grows and regenerates as we have the courage to let go and trust the process. Growth and joy are inhibited when we say "if only," enhanced when we realize that failures and difficulties are not only a critical part of the process, but are our very opportunity to grow.[5]

"If only..." This phrase makes us into people imprisoned in lost dreams. It's possible to keep yourself bottled up with "if onlys."

There's another phrase that can release us from this and usher us into the future. The phrase "Next time" shows that we have given up our regrets; we have learned from past occurrences and are getting on with our lives.

"What will I do?" This question is a cry of despair coupled with fear of the future and the unknown. In time we can learn to say, "I don't know what I can do at this moment, but I know I can handle this. Thank God I don't have to face this issue by myself. I can learn and become a different person."

We limit our growth and recovery by our beliefs and thoughts. For many people, the greatest prison is the locked door of their minds. We become performers and act out the rehearsed script in our minds.

Many years ago in a small town in the British Isles, a new jail was constructed that claimed to have an escape-proof cell. Harry Houdini, the world renowned escape artist, was invited to test it to see if it really was escape-proof. He accepted the invitation, having once boasted that no jail could hold him.

Houdini entered the cell, and the jailer closed the door behind him. Houdini listened to the sound of the key being slipped into the lock. The jailer withdrew the key and left. Houdini took out his tools and started the process of working on that cell door. But it didn't work out the way he expected. Nothing seemed to work, and the hours passed. He was puzzled because he'd never failed to open a locked door.

Finally the great Houdini admitted defeat. But when he leaned against the door in resigned exhaustion, it suddenly opened. The jailer had never locked the door. The only place the door was locked was—as you can guess—in Houdini's mind.

I've done it and so have you: we've locked ourselves in because of what we've thought and believed. As a result we lock ourselves away from being able to change. Instead of enjoying the assurance and freedom that come from belonging to God, we actually become the negative people we imagine ourselves to be.

If you are on the verge of giving up, you're probably familiar with the phrase, "I'm ready to throw in the towel!" Perhaps you've felt like saying it at one time or another in your life. You could say it now because you don't feel as though you have any more to give. As one man said, "There's nothing left for me to do. I feel empty. I don't have any hope left."

John Karetji, a pastor from Indonesia, says he made that statement during a difficult time in his life. A man came to him and asked if he knew where the phrase about throwing in the towel came from. He replied that he didn't. The man went on to tell him that it's a phrase used in boxing. When the manager standing outside the ring sees that his fighter can't make it any longer in the boxing match, he throws the towel into the ring, signifying they are giving up.

Did you notice? It's not the boxer who has the towel, it's the manager. Only the one who sent the boxer into the ring can throw in the towel.

We may feel like the boxer who wants to call it quits. But we were sent into the ring of life by someone else. *Remember who it was who sent you into the ring!* Jesus said, "I will never leave you nor forsake you," and "Lo, I am with you always."

Survivors Don't Become Bitter

Survivors *don't allow themselves to become bitter.* They refuse to live in the past or permit a situation to stop them in their tracks with no hope for the future. Bitterness comes from focusing on the unfairness of whatever has happened. It's like a warplane's radar locking onto a target. Bitterness leads to resentment, and the bitter person becomes the victim.

Many of the people I've seen who were stuck in their grief were there because of feelings of resentment. They built a dam around their bitterness instead of allowing it to drain away. Their resentment may have been against God, against their doctors, against the driver of the car that hit their son and left him in a coma, against the child who was into drugs. In each case they injured themselves and hindered their own growth more than anyone else's.

A man named Martin found this to be true while battling inoperable cancer. Here is his story:

> I am free, free, free! Free in spirit, free in
> mind, free in expression. Nothing in the

outer world can bind me or limit me. I am free from care, free to be happy, free to be loving and sharing today, free to be what God created me to be...

Jesus has shown me the why of suffering. I've found out that the person who must endure suffering will benefit from it if he is attentive to what the Lord is saying to him. As I look back over my life, I can personally testify that I could easily have done without many joyful experiences, but I could not have spared one valuable spiritual lesson I have learned from sorrow! Why? Because "God whispers in our pleasures but shouts in our pain"! The Lord forces us by our distresses to pay attention to His voice.

While such times of testing are not pleasant to endure, we must wait patiently for Him to accomplish His wise purposes. If we avoid becoming bitter in our earthly trials, we will learn the lessons of grace which only adversity can bring to the teachable heart. Those who accept troubles graciously grow rich by their losses, rise by their falls, and find new life in Christ by dying to self.

Often when God brings pressure into our lives, His purpose is to give us more power.[6]

Sometimes in discussing a painful situation, you hear someone say, "Don't tell me to forgive them! They don't deserve it!"

The natural response of anger and resentment causes pain, to be sure. And too often we choose to let it stay in our lives and gain a foothold. If your crisis involves another person, you may want to write a letter (don't mail it!) to either the event itself or the person involved. Write as much as you can each time under the headings "I resent..." and "I wish..." In time, your bitterness will lift, and that's the first step toward forgiveness. I've encouraged people to write letters to the company that fired them, the drunk driver of the car who killed a child, and the terrorists who destroyed the World Trade Center.

A similar problem that will keep a person and the entire family stuck in the past is an attitude of resignation: "I give up. Why try? Nothing will change. This will always be the problem." You believe you're defeated already, so you don't give God much room to work in the crisis or in your heart. There were times when I wondered about our daughter, "How long will this go on? It's been three years already!"

Sometimes resignation is reflected in martyrdom. Martyrs complain and sulk, have low-grade depression, or complain to just about anyone they meet about their difficulties. Unfortunately, in time this attitude will push others away.

Survivors Want to Learn and Grow

Survivors are those *who want to learn and grow.* They are overcomers.

In the book of Revelation, we find statements to the churches that are being judged. Each time there are words of great hope and encouragement given to "him who overcomes." It is to the overcomers that the Lord makes these promises (emphasis added):

> To him who *overcomes,* I will grant to eat from the tree of life, which is in the Paradise of God (2:7).

> He who *overcomes* shall not be hurt by the second death (2:11).

And he who *overcomes,* and he who keeps My deeds until the end, to him I will give authority over the nations...and I will give him the morning star (2:26-28).

He who *overcomes* shall thus be clothed in white garments; and I will not erase his name from the book of life, and I will confess his name before My Father, and before His angels (3:5).

He who *overcomes,* I will make him a pillar in the temple of My God, and he will not go out from it anymore; and I will write upon him the name of My God, and the name of the city of My God, the New Jerusalem, which comes down out of heaven from My God, and My new name (3:12).

He who *overcomes,* I will grant to him to sit with Me on My throne, as I also overcame and sat down with My Father on His throne (3:21).

Tom Sullivan has been a frequent guest on the *Good Morning America* program. He also did some guest appearances on *M*A*S*H** and *Fame* and had a part in *Airport '77*. Tom holds two national championship records in wrestling and was on the 1958 Olympic team for our country. He holds a degree from Harvard in clinical psychology; he is a musician and author, he runs six miles a day on the beach, he sky dives...and he is blind. That's right, Tom is blind. He can't see a thing. His life was portrayed in the gripping film *If You Could See What I Hear.*

When he speaks to large crowds, the audience is with him all the way, listening, applauding, laughing, and learning from a man who cannot see the enjoyment on their faces.

In his presentation, he has one major point: "You've got a disadvantage? Take advantage of it! People don't buy similarity. They buy differences." A disadvantage is what makes you stand out. Think about it. If you're similar to everyone else, you blend in and you're lost in the crowd.

Tom shared about the first time he realized he was blind. He was eight years old. He was in his backyard and he heard some new sounds—the crack of a bat as it hit a ball and the thud of the ball as it struck the outfielder's glove.

He listened some more and decided they were playing a game. Did he get discouraged because he was blind and couldn't see what was happening? Not at all. He found a rock and a stick and taught himself how to bat. He wasn't sure where to hit, so he devised a target to aim at. He set up a transistor radio on a tree stump, walked back a few steps, and began to practice. He practiced so much that eventually he could hit the radio every time.

After a while he told his dad that he wanted to play baseball. Imagine his father's reaction: "You want to do *what?*" Well actually, his dad said, "Really?...uh, which position?" Tom said, "I want to be a pitcher." Can you imagine the silence that hung in the air after that statement? His dad talked to the manager of the local Little League team and was able to get Tom on the team. And he pitched. They had another boy stand next to him to catch the ball when the catcher threw it back.

In Tom's presentation he says to the audience, "Can you picture this little frightened nine-year-old boy coming up to the plate, knowing that a blind kid is on the mound ready to throw a ball at him?" Eventually, after he knocked out several boys, he switched to wrestling. Probably a collective sigh of relief went up from every Little League team in town.

Tom has a great sense of humor and the ability to pop out his glass eyes. He claims he won a few wrestling matches that way.[7]

It's an amazing story. Tom had a choice between cynical self-pity or learning to live a courageous life. Each of us has the same choice. Listen to one last statement by this courageous man.

"I've determined that my disadvantage in life is blindness," Tom Sullivan says. "I will therefore become, as a blind person, all that I can possibly be. That will become my distinctive message."[8]

Survivors Live in the Present and Look to the Future

A characteristic of those who cope is that they *live in the present* and *have a future perspective*. They seek to learn from what has happened to them, not live with regrets. They also learn to view the future as an opportunity, not a threat.

Most of the opportunities that will arise in the future are completely unknown to us. As Dr. Lloyd Ogilvie says,

> The sure sign that we have an authentic relationship with God is that we believe more in the future than in the past. God graciously divided our life into days and years so that we could let go of yesterdays and anticipate our tomorrow. For our tomorrow, He gives us the gift of expectation and excitement.[9]

Holding on to *the truth of Scripture* and its promises will help individuals and families survive. God said, "Be strong and courageous! Do not tremble or be dismayed, for the LORD your God is with you wherever you go" (Joshua 1:9). He also promised, "For I know the plans that I have for you...plans for welfare and not for calamity to give you a future and a hope" (Jeremiah 29:11).

It's vital to look to the future, even with its unknowns, for that is what can guide what we do now. Dr. Paul Walker tells of his experience with a survivor who focused on the future:

> Do not worry about your life, what you will eat or drink; or about your body, what you will wear. Is not life more important than food, and the body more important than clothes? Look at the birds of the air; they do not sow or reap or store away into barns, and yet your heavenly Father feeds them. Are you not much more valuable than they? Who of you by worrying can add a single hour to his life? (Matthew 6:25-27 NIV).
>
> The key here is sanctification. The word sanctity means "to set apart and make holy." It is to consecrate and prepare for service. What this passage says is that as we sanctify our tomorrow we deal with the precious present. All we have is the now, and this now is to be lived out according to the highest priorities given to us by God in the fulfillment of the self. We are to allow tomorrow to take care of itself or, in other words, to commit the future into the hands of a loving God.
>
> This idea of sanctifying tomorrow was brought to me by a man who was dying with cancer. Throughout the whole ordeal of his sickness, he seemed to maintain a sense of enthusiasm and strength that was astounding. Time and time again he came near death, but each time he would rally, to the amazement of doctors, nurses, family and friends.

On one occasion I was called to the hospital because death was imminent. When I arrived, he was in a coma, and we all thought it was the end. But once again he endured and was able to return home.

During this period, I asked him, "How are you able to survive these close bouts with death? What is your secret?" In answer he said:

"When it became certain that I had an inoperable cancer, I made a deal with the Lord.

"First, I promised to live every moment of my life like it was the only moment I would have.

"Second, I sanctified all my tomorrows and put them in the Lord's hands for whatever He had planned.

"Third, I pray every day for a miracle of healing but know that I've got a good deal either way. If I receive a miracle, it will be a tremendous testimony to the world of God's great power and grace. If I die, I will go home to be with the Lord, and in reality that will be an even better deal.

"Whether I live or die, I can't lose!" [10]

Survivors Learn to Resolve Conflicts

One of the steps that helps families survive is learning to manage and resolve their conflicts. Families that don't do this heap one conflict upon another. When a new conflict occurs, their response is partially determined by their contaminated reservoir of unresolved issues. If you haven't learned to resolve conflicts before a crisis, you're not likely to do it during one.

When family members know conflicts aren't resolved, some may think, *Why even bother?* and not listen to others or engage them in conversation. A healthy family overrides its fears and discovers ways to make things different. Members learn to solve problems and are willing to listen to one another and try something new. This approach is a source of encouragement and hope in the midst of heartache.

It's also important to determine which problems are worth tackling, which are not, which ones can be resolved, and which cannot. At times, you'll need to postpone problem solving or take time out.

Successful families believe that each person has the ability to handle the adversity. They don't suffocate one another with words like "you should…" or "you ought to…" or by being overbearing with advice. Rather they encourage one another. Unconditional love is the backbone for their relationships.

Successful families also respect their members' personality differences. If a person needs to talk or do something— or needs privacy and quiet—that's all right.

Survivors Enjoy Life

Those who survive crisis have an established pattern of *enjoying life*. They can laugh even during the difficult times. It's a way of taking a break from the heaviness of the crisis.

The first time I experienced this was as a youth pastor when I led a group of 25 high schoolers on a camping trip into the high Sierra Mountain Range in southern California. One morning two of the boys set out on their own to climb the face of a sheer rock protruding hundreds of feet into the sky. One of the boys fell 400 feet to his death. For hours a sense of heavy gloom lay on all of us. After dinner the campers began cracking jokes and were laughing and joking for over an hour. Other adults wondered, "How could they?" But those kids needed to take that break. We all do at times.

A wife shared her story about the value of humor:

> We try to treat things seriously that need it and poke fun at the rest. We often ask ourselves, "Will this be funny later?" and lots of petty irritants are. I'll give you an example. We headed out for a company potluck dinner one evening in a bit of a fluster because we were about five minutes late, and my husband was supposed to give the invocation. At the car trunk, juggling the keys and a casserole, he spilled the hot casserole on his hand and down his trousers. He flipped it onto the lawn (killing the grass, by the way) and raced back inside to change clothes. We raced off and were halfway there when a police officer pulled us over. We had missed a new "No left turn" sign at an intersection. Of course the officer wanted to see my husband's license, and you know where his wallet was? Right! At home in the other trousers. There we sat explaining spilled casseroles and changed clothes to the officer. She let us go with a warning. No one could have made up a story like ours. We arrived at the dinner and my husband said, "I'm sorry we're late, but I am very thankful just to be here. Let me tell you why..." His humor changed a blood-pressure-raising series of incidents into a good story.

One final example comes from our friend Sally, a courageous woman who was born with a rare degenerative disease that slowly constricts her body. She spends time in a wheelchair and was in danger of dying when we talked with her. Her spine had bent so much that she was down to 30 percent of her normal breathing capacity. She was slowly suffocating.

A major operation was her only hope; her back would be cut open from top to bottom and stainless steel inserts put into each vertebra to help straighten her spine. "Normal" life in which one walks and runs would never be possible, but life itself would be possible.

As we talked, she joked about being a "bionic woman" and predicted that she would need a whole new wardrobe. When asked why, she answered, "Because I'll be six-foot-seven with all those metal spacers in me. And think of what havoc I'll cause in airport metal detectors!"

"Seriously, Sally," we asked, "how can you laugh so much about this?"

"You know what they say," she replied. "It's either laugh or cry."

Laughter often is the balm we need for the silliness, madness, and ironies of daily life.[11]

Survivors Adapt to Change

Survivors are *flexible, resilient, and adaptable.* The lack of these qualities makes a huge difference in the way a person copes with life. In other words, the more rigid a person is, the less hopeful his life is, because rigidity makes changing direction difficult. Perfectionists and those who must have everything under control have a hard time handling crises. How do you think others would describe you? Do you think they would say you are rigid or flexible? Ask your spouse or a trusted friend if you're unsure of the answer.

Sometimes we think of survivors as being extraordinary individuals. A few are, but most are not. Survivors—people of hope and faith—have their faults and flaws. They are like anyone else, with one exception. They have a different way of thinking about some things. Here's a reminder of some of the attitudes that characterize survivors.

1. *The survivor says, "I will examine the future and let it guide what I do in the present."* Many people, upon reaching middle age or old age, move into despair. They have regrets over the way they have lived, or they realize there's little time left to change things. Perhaps by examining our priorities and values at a younger age we can gain better direction for our lives and be satisfied in later years.

According to the Scriptures, living life with a forward view is healthy and hopeful. Jesus said,

> Most assuredly, I say to you, he who believes in Me, the works that I do he will do also; and greater works than these he will do, because I go to My Father. And whatever you ask in My name, that I will do, that the Father may be glorified in the Son. If you ask anything in My name, I will do it.
>
> JOHN 14:12-14 NKJV

God asked Abraham to look into the future. In Genesis 13:14-16, He instructed Abraham to gaze northward, southward, eastward, and westward at the land He was giving to him. Then in verse 17 God told Abraham, then called Abram, to do something very strange: "Arise, walk in the land through its length and width; for I will give it to you."

Dr. Lloyd Ogilvie comments:

> In order to build in Abram the confidence of a risk taker, the Lord had to help him claim the reality of the seemingly impossible. He not only gave him a vision, but he also made

him walk through that vision until he made it really his own.

God does the same thing with you and me. First he gives us the impossible dream, then he helps us envision what it will be like to possess our possession, and then through our imagination he helps us persistently imagine the reality. What is the dream for you?

Have you examined your future? Will you today?

2. *The survivor says, "No matter what happens, I will not allow myself to be defeated. I will keep on trying and will not give up."* Perseverance is a mark of hope and faith. It is essential to realizing God's blessing. Do you persevere and keep on trying?

3. *The survivor says, "I am a fortunate person, regardless of what I have experienced."* You may be ignoring the blessings around you by focusing on your losses instead of your gains. There is always hope and the possibility of growth. You could be much worse off than you are. Survivors consistently take inventory of what they have rather than what they do not have. When was the last time you took such an inventory?

4. *The survivor says, "I will take advantage of every available opportunity."* I have spoken with disabled people who look for every opportunity to create and grow. Perhaps the more disabled someone is, the more he appreciates what he can experience. We all need to look at life through thankful eyes and seize the opportunity around us. What opportunities are around you right now that you could take advantage of and use to generate even more hope for yourself?

5. *The survivor says, "I can accept my imperfections and learn to enjoy life and give to others."* Survivors don't strive for perfection; they realize it's impossible to be perfect. But they do work toward excellence. What are your imperfections? Do you dwell on these deficits, or do you direct your energy toward improving what can be improved while accepting what can't be changed?

6. *The survivor says, "I can find meaning in situations and events that involve suffering or great loss."* Where meaninglessness exists, there is no hope. Sometimes the meaning of a negative or hurtful event cannot be seen until much later. Over a period of 22 years, my wife and I learned this lesson and this attitude through the life and death of our son, Matthew.

You must grieve your losses and then come to the point of replacing the "why" questions with the "how" questions: "How can I learn through this experience? How can I grow through this? How can God be glorified through this experience?"

7. *The survivor says, "I will not allow myself to behave as a victim."* Even in the midst of the hurt and pain of life, survivors learn to move on, and they choose not to see themselves as helpless victims. For most people, this involves a change in thinking. Do you see yourself as a victim? If so, does this attitude create more victim experiences for you?

8. *The survivor says, "I'm determined to keep pushing ahead."* Survivors are able to make and keep commitments. They are able to build their lives on Jeremiah 29:11 and 33:3 and allow God to guide them: "For I know the thoughts that I think toward you, says the LORD, thoughts of peace and not of evil, to give you a future and a hope" (NKJV); "Call to Me, and I will answer you, and show you great and mighty things, which you do not know" (NKJV). In what ways are

you living in the past? In what ways are you purposefully moving ahead in life?

9. *The survivor says, "I am willing to grow, change, and learn new roles."* I often see this attitude in divorced persons as they learn to function as both mom and dad to their children. I see this in men who are able to learn to be affectionate, demonstrative, and feeling oriented in relationships. Every one of us has an opportunity to grow. If we don't, our only option is stagnation. In what ways are you growing and changing? In what ways do you need to expand in order to help yourself and those around you?

10. *The survivor says, "I want to be involved with people who will build me up and help me grow."* We were never meant to make it alone. But it's foolish to surround ourselves with people who fill our mind with negative talk and example. We can't grow and be blessed if we spend all our time with sick people.

Healthy people don't tear you down or drain you. You need people in your life to give you strength. You need encouragers. Who are the significant people in your life, and in what ways do they help you mature and grow stronger? Who do you pray for? Who prays for you?

11. *The survivor says, "I can face the challenges of life and handle the stresses and crises of life without denying their existence or giving up."* I especially like this attitude of a survivor. It's not just what happens to us; it's how we respond to what happens to us that's so important. It's the ability to take James 1:2-3 and apply it to our lives. Remember, a survivor is a person who makes sense out of what happens to him or her. Never, never let go of your hope.[12]

I have a friend afflicted by multiple sclerosis. During the beginning years of his disease, he experienced the pain of divorce as well. In 1990, when he was still somewhat ambulatory, he married a woman 14 years younger. In preparation for their life together with a disease that would become progressively worse, they both attended several national conferences on multiple sclerosis to learn as much as they could about what to expect in the future. Lisa began cooking his specialized diet even before their marriage. They discussed issues they thought they would face in the future, including their ages, who would eventually support the family, and whether or not to have children.

Having prepared for the kind of life neither one would have chosen, they made a success of their life together. They had two children and Dave worked at home after retiring on disability insurance from his previous job. Lisa teaches school until noon and then returns home. I asked Dave, "How have you made it? How do you go on?" This is what he told me:

> First of all, it is my relationship with the Lord. My faith in Him has sustained me. Then it's been Lisa. In our wedding vows she pledged to be my hands and feet. And more and more she's doing this. I've learned to make adjustments to my life for what I could no longer do. It was difficult to respond to letters and E-mail with my computer. So I was able to obtain a voice-activated computer, and I'm able to be as verbal as ever in my responses.
>
> Another factor has been the memorizing of God's Word. I recite the verses out loud, which strengthens my mouth muscles. With MS, your speech tends to get sloppy, and doing this helps to keep this from occurring. You lose so many abilities as it is with MS. Each time you lose one you have to fight the tendency to give up on everything. When

> each ability goes you have to grieve over that
> loss just like you did before. You never finish
> the process of grieving throughout this. But
> memorizing God's Word gives you the inner
> strength and confidence as well as depend-
> ing upon the Lord.

Do you see all the factors involved in this man's survival?
Dave's faith in God and his reliance upon others, especially
his wife, were strong factors in overcoming his disabilities.
Dave wouldn't give up. He moved ahead with his life with
a new family, making adjustments, discovering new ways to
function, relying upon God's Word, and facing his losses by
grieving over them. This is what it takes to move on in life.

I love the following prayer by Chuck Swindoll, and
encourage you to make it yours:

> It's not often, Father, that we make such a
> statement, but today we thank You for the
> injustices that have crippled us and broken
> us and crushed us. We want to express our
> appreciation for the things that have brought
> us to the place of submission. The only way
> we can look is up.
>
> We express our gratitude for the things
> You have taught us through blindness and
> loss and paralysis; for growth through
> broken dreams, dissolved partnerships, ill-
> ness, and sadness; for the character devel-
> opment through insecurity, failure, and even
> divorce. We see the storm, but we are begin-
> ning to see You beyond the storm. How
> essential is our attitude!
>
> Thank you especially for helping us con-
> quer our cynicism.

I pray for those in these and a hundred other categories, that we may be able to go beyond them and find in Jesus Christ the strength to go on, especially for those who, only a few moments ago, had just about decided to give up. I pray that they will rather give it all to You in full surrender.

In the strong name of Jesus Christ, the Conqueror, I pray. Amen.[13]

Hope Makes a Difference

Hope looks for the good in people instead of harping on the worst in them.

Hope opens doors where despair closes them.

Hope discovers what can be done instead of grumbling about what cannot be done.

Hope draws its power from a deep trust in God and the basic goodness of mankind.

Hope "lights a candle" instead of "cursing the darkness."

Hope regards problems, small or large, as opportunities.

Hope cherishes no illusions, nor does it yield to cynicism.

                    Source Unknown

Appendix:
Moving Toward Recovery

At some point it's important to be able to evaluate where you are in your grief process. Dr. Therese Rando, who has made an outstanding contribution to the study of grief and recovery, suggests that we should evaluate recovery by observing changes in ourselves, in our relationship with what we have lost, and in our relationships with the world and other people.[1] It often helps to go through this evaluation with a person who can assist you with an objective viewpoint.

As you read and answer the following evaluation statements, your conclusions may help you to decide where you are in your recovery.

On a scale of 0-10 (0 meaning "not at all" and 10 meaning "total recovery in that area"), rate yourself in response to each question. This evaluation is geared toward the loss of a person, but it can be adapted to other losses as well.

Changes Because of My Loss

I have returned to my normal levels of functioning in most areas of my life.

0——————————5——————————10

My overall symptoms of grief have declined.

0——————————5——————————10

My feelings do not overwhelm me when I think about my loss or when someone mentions it.

0———————————5———————————10

Most of the time I feel all right about myself.

0———————————5———————————10

I enjoy myself and what I experience without feeling guilty.

0———————————5———————————10

My anger has diminished, and when it occurs, I handle it appropriately.

0———————————5———————————10

I don't avoid thinking about things that could be or are painful.

0———————————5———————————10

My hurt has diminished and I understand it.

0———————————5———————————10

I can think of positive things.

0———————————5———————————10

I have completed what I need to do about my loss.

0———————————5———————————10

My pain does not dominate my thoughts or my life.

0———————————5———————————10

I can handle special days or dates without feeling totally overwhelmed by memories.

0———————————5———————————10

I have handled the secondary losses that accompanied my major loss.

0———————————5———————————10

I can remember the loss on occasion without pain
and without crying.

0————————————5————————————10

There is meaning and significance to my life.

0————————————5————————————10

I am able to ask how rather than why at this time.

0————————————5————————————10

I see hope and purpose in life in spite of my loss.

0————————————5————————————10

I have energy and can feel relaxed during the day.

0————————————5————————————10

I no longer fight the fact that the loss has occurred.
I have accepted it.

0————————————5————————————10

I am learning to be comfortable with my new identity
and in being without what I lost.

0————————————5————————————10

I understand that my feelings over the loss will return
periodically, and I can understand and accept that.

0————————————5————————————10

I understand what grief means and have a greater
appreciation for it.

0————————————5————————————10

Changes in My Relationship with the Person I Lost

I remember our relationship realistically with positive and negative memories.

0————————5————————10

The relationship I have with the person I lost is healthy and appropriate.

0————————5————————10

I feel all right about not thinking about the loss for a time. I don't feel as though I am betraying the one I lost.

0————————5————————10

I have a new relationship with the person I have lost. I know appropriate ways of keeping the person "alive."

0————————5————————10

I no longer go on a search for my loved one.

0————————5————————10

I don't feel compelled to hang on to the pain.

0————————5————————10

The ways I keep memories of my loved one alive are healthy and acceptable.

0————————5————————10

I can think about things in life other than what I lost.

0————————5————————10

My life has meaning even though this person is gone.

0————————5————————10

Changes I Have Made in Adjusting to My New World

I have integrated my loss into my world and I can relate to others in a healthy way.

0————————————5————————————10

I can accept the help and support of other people.

0————————————5————————————10

I am open about my feelings in other relationships.

0————————————5————————————10

I feel it is all right for life to go on even though my loved one is gone.

0————————————5————————————10

I have developed an interest in people and things outside myself that have no relationship to the person I lost.

0————————————5————————————10

I have put the loss in perspective.

0————————————5————————————10[2]

Grief recovery is a back-and-forth process. One of the better ways to identify your progress is through a personal journal. Writing down your thoughts will give you proof that you are making progress even though your feelings say otherwise. Your journal is your own private property and is not for anyone else to read. It is an expression of what you are feeling and your climb to recovery. It can be written in any style—simple statements, poems, or prayers that reflect your journey. The authors of *The Grief Adjustment Guide* offer some helpful suggestions for keeping a journal.

1. You may find it helpful to make time every day to write at least a short paragraph in your journal. At the end of a week, review what you have written to see small steps of progress toward grief recovery. Writing at least

a line or two every day is the most effective way to keep a journal.

2. Some people write in their journals a few times each week, reviewing the entries at the end of the week and at the end of each month. If you have trouble getting started, look over the following list of suggested beginnings. Find one that fits what you are feeling or need to express and use it to "jump start" your writing for that day:

1. My biggest struggle right now is...
2. The thing that really gets me down is...
3. The worst thing about my loss is...
4. When I feel lonely...
5. The thing I fear most...
6. The most important thing I've learned is...
7. The thing that keeps me from moving on is...
8. I seem to cry most when...
9. I dreamed last night...
10. I heard a song that reminded me of...
11. A new person I've come to appreciate is...
12. I get angry when...
13. Part of the past that keeps haunting me is...
14. What I've learned from the past is...
15. Guilt feelings seem to come most when...
16. The experiences I miss the most are...
17. New experiences I enjoy the most are...
18. The changes I least and most like are...
19. My feelings sometimes confuse me because...
20. I smelled or saw something today that reminded me of...
21. A new hope I found today is...
22. New strengths I've developed since my loss are...
23. I feel close to God today because...
24. I am angry at God today because...
25. For me to find and have balance, I...

26. I got a call or letter from a friend today that…
27. My friend, _____, had a loss today, and I…[3]

If one of these doesn't fit, then write about what you are feeling. You could start with just one word—*misery, longing, hope,* or whatever—and then describe that feeling with phrases or sentences. If you need to, cry as you write, but keep writing until there is nothing more to say about that feeling.

Your journal is your place to say and feel what is in your heart and mind. It is your way of crystallizing the feelings of loss. Dealing with your feelings one at a time in a written, tangible form is a good way to "own" those feelings and respond to them in an organized way. Grief is a whole tangle of feelings, and writing them down is a great way to isolate and adjust to each one.

Monitor what you write. When you begin to see yourself writing more about what is happening *today* and less about the one you have lost, you'll know that healing and adjustment are indeed taking place, though it may seem painfully slow. Look for signs of progress.

It is *your* journal; use it for your own benefit.[4]

Perhaps the chart on the next page will assist you in your journey of recovery. Use it with the accompanying evaluation questions.

1. Cross out the stages you have already experienced.
2. List ways you have freed yourself from being "stuck" in one phase.
3. Make some statements to yourself about your own patterns of handling loss experiences. (Examples: "I turn inward instead of outward." "I internalize my anger.")
4. List the strengths you now have because of the grief you have experienced. (Examples: "I'm a survivor!" "I've learned empathy for others.")
5. What are some ways you can use these new strengths to help others?[5]

Notes

Chapter 1

1. Dave Dravecky with Tim Stafford, *Comeback* (Grand Rapids, MI: Zondervan, 1990), adapted, p. 16.
2. Gerald Sittser, *A Grace Disguised* (Grand Rapids, MI: Zondervan, 1996), pp. 17-18.
3. Langston Hughes, as quoted in Ann Kaiser Stearns, *Living Through Personal Crisis* (Chicago: Thomas Moore, 1984), p. 25.
4. Marilyn Willet Heavelin, *When Your Dreams Die* (San Bernardino, CA: Here's Life, 1990), pp. 30-31.

Chapter 2

1. Max Lucado, *In the Eye of the Storm* (Dallas: Word, 1991), pp. 105-106.
2. Lewis Smedes, *How Can It Be All Right When Everything Is All Wrong?* (San Francisco: Harper & Row, 1982), pp. 55-56.
3. Charles Swindoll, *Growing Strong in the Seasons of Life* (Portland, OR: Multnomah, 1983), pp. 274-275.
4. Alexander Solzhenitsyn, as quoted in Barry Johnson, *Choosing Hope* (Nashville: Abingdon, 1988), p. 178.
5. Johnson, p. 178.
6. Sittser, pp. 62-63.

Chapter 3

1. Ann Kaiser Stearns, *Coming Back* (New York: Random House, 1988), pp. 85-86.
2. Gordon MacDonald, as quoted in Gary J. Oliver, *How to Get It All Right After You've Gotten It All Wrong* (Wheaton, IL: Victor, 1995), p. 48.
3. Gordon MacDonald, as quoted in Oliver, p. 48.
4. Pauline Boss, *Ambiguous Loss* (Harvard University Press, 1999).
5. Boss, p. 6.
6. Boss, p. 10.
7. Aaron Lazare et al., "The Walk-In Patient as a 'Customer': A Key Dimension in Evaluation and Treatment," *American Journal of Orthopsychiatry,* 42, (1979), pp. 872-883.
8. Max Lucado, *In the Eye of the Storm* (Dallas: Word, 1991), adapted, pp. 193-194.
9. Frederick Buechner, *Peculiar Treasures: A Biblical Who's Who* (New York: Harper & Row, 1979), p. 65.
10. Erin Lim, *I Know Just How You Feel: Avoid the Cliches of Grief* (Gary, IN: Publishers Mark, 1986), xii, xiii.
11. William Pruitt, *Run from the Pale Pony* (Grand Rapids, MI: Baker, 1976), pp. 9-10.

Chapter 4

1. Information has been adapted from the following articles: "New Hope, New Dreams" by Roger Rosen Platt, *Time* August 6, 1996 v 148, N10, p. 40 (13); "Fighting to Fund an Absolute Necessity" by Kendall Hamilton, *Newsweek,* July 1, 1996, v. 128, N1, p. 56 (1); "We Draw Strength from Each Other" by Liz Smith, *Good Housekeeping,* June 1996, v. 322, N6, p. 86 (5).
2. Carol Staudacher, *Beyond Grief* (Oakland, CA: New Harbinger, 1987), adapted, pp. 10-31.

3. Earl A. Grolman, *Living When a Loved One Has Died* (Boston: Beacon Press, 1987), adapted, pp. 39-41.
4. Shirley Inrau, "Learning with a Dying Mother," *Confident Living,* December 1987, pp. 20-22. Used by permission of the author.
5. Maggie Scarf, *Unfinished Business: Pressure Points in the Lives of Women* (New York: Doubleday, 1985), pp. 86-87.
6. David W. Willske, *Gone but Not Lost* (Grand Rapids, MI: Baker, 1992), adapted, p. 55.

Chapter 5
1. Therese A. Rando, *Grieving: How to Go on Living When Someone You Love Dies* (Lexington, MA: Lexington Books, 1988), adapted, pp. 556-557.
2. Rando, p. 44.
3. Therese A. Rando, *Treatment of Complicated Mourning* (Champaign, IL: Research Press, 1983), p. 512.
4. Glen W. Davidson, *Understanding Mourning* (Minneapolis, MN: Augsburg, 1984), p. 59.
5. Joyce and Norm Wright, *I'll Love You Forever* (Colorado Springs, CO: Focus on the Family, 1993), adapted, pp. 69-76.
6. Wright, adapted, pp. 138-50.
7. Wright, pp. 41, 42, 44, 45.
8. Susan J. Zonnebelt-Smeege and R.N.: ED.D. and Robert C. DeVries, D.Min: Ph.D., *Getting to the Other Side of Grief* (Grand Rapids, MI: Baker Book House, 2001), p. 13.
9. Zonnebelt-Smeege and DeVries, p. 16-17.
10. Delores Kuenning, *Helping People Through Grief* (Minneapolis, MN: Bethany House, 1987), adapted, pp. 227-228.
11. Ken Gire, *Windows of the Soul* (Grand Rapids, MI: Zondervan, 1996), p. 140.

Chapter 6
1. John W. James and Russell Friedman, *When Children Grieve* (New York: HarperCollins, 2001), p. 5.
2. J. Williams Worden, *Children and Grief, When a Parent Dies* (New York: Guildford Press, 1996), adapted, p. 134.
3. H. Norman Wright, *Crisis Counseling* (Ventura, CA: Regal Books, 1993), pp. 202-203.
4. Maryann Emswiler, M.A., M.P.S. and James P. Emswiler, M.A., M.Ed., *Guiding Your Child Through Grief* (New York: Bantam Books, 2000), adapted, pp. 100-106.
5. Carol Staudacher, *Beyond Grief* (Oakland, CA: New Harbinger Publications, 1987), adapted, pp. 129-130.
6. William Van Ornum and John B. Mordock, *Crisis Counseling with Children and Adolescents* (New York: Continuum, 1983), pp. 21-33.
7. Dan Schaefer and Christine Lyons, *How Do We Tell the Children?* (New York: New Market Press, 1986) p. 122.
8. Therese A. Rando, *Grieving* (Lexington, MA: Lexington Books, 1988), adapted, pp. 200-204.

Chapter 7
1. Dan Schaefer and Christine Lyons, *How Do We Tell the Children?* (New York: New Market Press, 1986) p. 129.
2. Carol Staudacher, *Beyond Grief* (Oakland, CA: New Harbinger, 1987), pp. 131-138.
3. J. William Worden, *Children and Grief, When a Parent Dies* (New York: Guildford Press, 1996), pp. 33-34.
4. Schaefer and Lyons, pp. 33-34.
5. Worden, pp. 33-34.
6. Schaefer and Lyons, pp. 124-125.
7. Staudacher, pp. 146-147.
8. Staudacher, p. 151.
9. Therese A. Rando, *Grieving* (Lexington, MA: Lexington Books, 1988), p. 218.
10. Linda Jane Volga, *Helping a Child Understand Death* (Philadelphia, PA: Fortress Press, 1975), pp. 63-64.

11. Schaefer and Lyons, p. 142.
12. Rando, adapted, p. 218.
13. Staudacher, pp. 138-139.

Chapter 8

1. Donald Meichenbaum, *A Clinical Handbook/Practiced; Therapist Manual for Assessing and Treating Adults with Post Traumatic Stress Disorder (PTSD)* (Waterloo, Ont.: Institute Press, 1994), adapted, p. 23.
2. Elie Wiesel, "Parade Magazine," *Los Angeles Times*, Oct. 2001, pp. 4,5.
3. Sandra L. Brown, *Counseling Victims of Violence* (Alexandria, VA: American Association for Counseling and Development, 1991), adapted, p. 9.
4. Diane Langberg, quoted from a presentation for the TRIP Conference, New York City, Oct. 2001, adapted.
5. Meichenbaum, adapted, pp. 510-511.
6. Aphrodite Matsakis, *I Can't Get Over It: A Handbook for Trauma Survivors* (Oakland, CA: New Harbinger, 1992), adapted, pp. 6-7.
7. Matsakis, adapted, pp. 23-24.
8. Matsakis, adapted, pp. 10-13.
9. Langberg.
10. Robert Hicks, *Failure to Scream* (Nashville; Nelson, 1993), p. 21.
11. C. S. Lewis, *A Grief Observed* (London: Fober & Fober, 1961), p. 9.
12. Brown, adapted, pp. 22-24.
13. C.S. Lewis, "Relapse," *Poems,* Walter Hooper, ed. (New York: Harcourt Brace Jovanovich, 1964), pp. 103-104.
14. Hicks, adapted, p. 46.
15. Matsakis, adapted, pp. 18-22.
16. Raymond B. Flammery, Jr., *Post-Traumatic Stress Disorder* (New York: Crossroad, 1992), adapted, pp. 36-37.
17. Terence Monmaney, "For Most Trauma Victims Life is More Meaningful, *LA Times*, Sunday Oct. 7, 2001, p. 9. Citing research from Richard Tedeschi, University of North Carolina; Dr. Robert Ursano, Uniformed Services University of the Health Sceiences in Bethesda, MD; Dr. Sandra Bloom.
18. Matsakis, adapted, p. 134.
19. Matsakis, adapted, pp. 15, 153.
20. Matsakis, adapted, p. 159.
21. Matsakis, adapted, pp. 160-263.
22. Matsakis, adapted, p. 236.

Chapter 9

1. Lloyd J. Ogilvie, *If God Cares, Why Do I Still Have Problems?* (Waco, TX: Word, 1985), adapted, p. 18.
2. Gary Kinnaman, *My Companion Through Grief* (Ann Arbor, MI: Servant, 1996), p. 17.
3. Ronald Dunn, *When Heaven Is Silent* (Nashville, TN: Thomas Nelson, 1994), pp. 113-114.
4. Dwight Carlson, *When Life Isn't Fair* (Eugene, OR: Harvest House, 1989); Harold Kushner, *When Bad Things Happen to Good People* (New York: Avon Books, 1981), p. 129.
5. C.S. Lewis, *The Problem of Pain* (London: Collins, 1961), p. 36.
6. Daniel Simundson, *Where Is God in Our Suffering?* (Minneapolis: Augsbury, 1983), p. 29, quoted in Delores Kuenning, *Helping People Through Grief* (Minneapolis: Bethany House, 1987).
7. Lewis Smedes, *How Can It Be All Right When Everything Is All Wrong?* (San Francisco: Harper and Row, 1982), p. 56.
8. Smedes, pp. 57-59.
9. Sittser, adapted, pp. 113-114.
10. Sittser, adapted, pp. 114-115.
11. Philip Yancey, *Where Is God When It Hurts?* (New York: Harper & Row, 1977), p. 89.
12. Carlson, p. 38.
13. Carlson, p. 43.

14. G. Tom Milazzo, *The Protest and the Silence* (Minneapolis: Fortress, 1992), p. 43.
15. Scott Peck, *People of the Lie* (New York: Simon & Schuster, 1983), adapted, p. 41.
16. Dunn, adapted, pp. 62-64.
17. Don Baker, *Pain's Hidden Purpose* (Portland, OR: Multnomah, 1984), p. 72.
18. Larry Richards, *When It Hurts Too Much* (Dallas: Word, 1985), pp. 67-68.
19. Yancey, pp. 206-207.

Chapter 10

1. Lucado, p. 11, adapted.
2. Tim Hansel, *You Gotta Keep Dancin'* (Colorado Springs, CO: David C. Cook, 1985), pp. 90-91.
3. Dr. Joy Joffe, as quoted in Stearns, p. 62.
4. Dr. Gerald Mann, original source unknown.
5. Charlie and Lucy Wedemeyer, *Charlie's Victory* (Grand Rapids, MI: Zondervan, 1993), p. 20.
6. Gire, pp. 193-194.
7. Gire, p. 195.
8. Hicks, pp. 11-12.

Chapter 11

1. Robert Veninga, *A Gift of Hope* (Boston: Little Brown & Co., 1985), adapted, pp. 66-70.
2. Veninga, p. 71.
3. Wayne Monbleau, *You Don't Find Water on the Mountain Top* (Grand Rapids, MI: Revell, 1996), pp. 58-59.
4. Paul Walker, *How to Keep Your Joy* (Nashville, TN: Thomas Nelson, 1987), pp. 58-59.
5. Hansel, pp. 132-133.
6. Walker, p. 23.
7. Tom Sullivan, adapted from a speech given to the Million Dollar Round Table Annual Meeting, 1983.
8. Sullivan.
9. Lloyd J. Ogilvie, *God's Best for My Life* (Eugene, OR: Harvest House, 1981), p. 9.
10. Walker, pp. 98-99.
11. Nick Stinnett and John DeFran, *Secrets of Strong Families* (Boston: Little Brown and Co., 1985), pp. 140-141.
12. Stearns, pp. 58-179.
13. Charles Swindoll, *Living on the Ragged Edge*, Word Books, Waco, TX; 1990, pp. 110-111.

Appendix

1. Rando, *Grieving,* adapted, pp. 281-283.
2. Rando, *Grieving,* adapted, pp. 284-286.
3. Charlotte Greeson, Mary Hollingsworth, and Michael Washburn, *The Grief Adjustment Guide* (Sisters, OR: Questar, 1990), pp. 90-91.
4. Greeson, Hollingsworth, and Washburn, pp. 90-91.
5. Greeson, Hollingsworth, and Washburn, p. 68, and H. Norman Wright, *Recovering from the Losses of Life,* (Grand Rapids, MI: Fleming H. Revell, 2001), adapted, pp. 115-122.

Acknowledgments

Materials taken from *You Gotta Keep Dancin'* by Tim Hansel, Chariot Victor Publishing, ©1986. Used by permission of Chariot Victor Publishing.

Materials taken from *Depression and the Integrated Life* by Richard. R. Berg and Dr. Christine McCartney, ©1981. Used by permission of Alba House.

Materials taken from *Transitions through Adult Life* by Charles M. Sell. © 1985 by Moody Bible Institute. Used by permission of Zondervan Publishing House.

Materials taken from *Family Shock* by Gary R. Collins, ©1995. Used by permission of Tyndale House Publishers, Inc. All rights reserved.

Materials taken from *Unfinished Business* by Maggie Scarf, Bantam/Doubleday Publishing, ©1985. Used by permission of Bantam/Doubleday Publishing.

Materials taken from *The Protest and the Silence* by G. Tom Milazzo, Augsburg Fortress, ©1992. Used by permission of Augsburg Fortress.

Materials taken from *When Life Isn't Fair* by Dwight Carlson, ©1989 by Harvest House Publishers, Eugene, Oregon. Used by permission.

Materials taken from *How to Get It Right After You've Gotten It Wrong* by Gary Oliver, Chariot Victor Publishing, ©1995. Used by permission of Chariot Victor Publishing.

Materials taken from *Counseling Teenagers* by G. Keith Olson, ©1984. Published by Group Publishing, Inc., Box 481 Loveland, CO 80539. *Resource: Lazare, Aaron, Cohen, F., Jacobsen, O., et.al. "The Walk-in Patient as a 'Customer': A Key Dimension in Evaluation and Treatment"*

American Journal of Orthopsychiatry, 42 (1979), pp. 872-883.

Materials taken from *Windows of the Soul*, by Ken Gire. ©1996 by Ken Gire, Jr. Used by permission of Zondervan Publishing House.

Materials taken from *Where is God When It Hurts?* by Philip Yancey. ©1977, 1990 by Philip Yancey. Used by permission of Zondervan Publishing House.

Materials taken from *In the Eye of the Storm* by Max Lucado, ©1991, Word, Inc., Dallas, Texas. Used by permission. All rights reserved.

Materials taken from *Making Love Last Forever* by Gary Smalley, ©1996, Word, Inc., Dallas, Texas. Used by permission. All rights reserved.

Materials taken from *Coming Back* by Ann Kaiser Stearns, ©1988 by Ann Kaiser Stearns. Reprinted by permission of Ballantine.

Materials taken from *When It Hurts Too Much to Wait* by Larry Richards, ©1985. Used by permission of Larry Richards.

Materials taken from *When Your Dreams Die* by Marilyn Wilett Heavelin, © 1990; *Facing Fifty* by Jim Smoke, ©1994; *Two Part Harmony* by Patrick Mosley, ©1994; *Failure to Scream* by Robert Hicks, ©1993; and *How to Keep Your Joy* by Paul Walker, ©1987. All published by Thomas Nelson Publishers. Used by permission.

Materials taken from *Beyond Endurance* by Robert Knapp, ©1986.

Materials taken from *You Don't Find Water on the Mountain Top* by Wayne Monbleau, ©1996.

Materials taken from *Living When a Loved One Has Died* by Earl Gralbman, ©1987.

Materials taken from *Secrets of Strong Families* by Nick Stinnett and John DeFran ©1985.

Materials taken from *When Bad Things Happen to Good People* by Harold Kushner, ©1981.

Materials taken from *The Finishing Touch* by Charles Swindoll, © 1995.

Materials taken from *A Grace Disguised* by Gerald L. Sittser, ©1996 by Gerald L. Sittser. Used by permission of Zondervan Publishing House.

Materials taken from *Run from the Pale Pony* by William Pruitt ©1976.